Andy Murray

THE

SCOTTISH VISITORS' ALMANAC

LOCHAR PUBLISHING · MOFFAT · SCOTLAND

For Adam

© Andy Murray, 1991

Published by Lochar Publishing Ltd
Moffat DG10 9ED

British Library Cataloguing in Publication Data
Murray, Andy
    The Scottish visitors' almanac.
    1. Scotland – Visitors' guides
    I. Title
    914.1104859

ISBN 0-948403-58-6

Typeset in 8½ on 9pt Times by Chapterhouse, Formby,
and printed in Scotland by Eagle Colour Books, Blantyre.

CONTENTS

ACKNOWLEDGMENTS

The Publishers would like to thank the following for providing illustrations:

Culzean Castle, Jarlshof, Edinburgh City Chambers, Edinburgh Royal Botanic Garden, Famous Old Blacksmith Shop Gretna Green, Inveraray Jail, Grandholm Mills, Finlaystone Estate, Chivas Brothers Ltd, Biggar Museum Trust, Traquair House, Helen Riley, Invergordon Distillers Ltd, Inverewe Gardens, John Knox House, Baxters of Speyside Ltd, Clan Donald Centre, New Lanark Village, Glasgow Botanic Gardens, David Livingstone Centre, Scotch Whisky Heritage Centre, Balmoral, Glasgow Art Gallery and Museum, National Trust for Scotland, Glamis Castle, Nature Conservancy Council South West Region Scotland, Buccleuch Recreational Enterprises Ltd, John Walker & Sons Ltd, Historic Scotland, Chambers Cox PR, Donald Clements, Abbotsford, Arbroath Abbey, Robert Anderson, Aden Country Park, Aberdeen Art Gallery, The Edinburgh Butterfly Farm Ltd, Cawdor Castle, Official Loch Ness Monster Exhibition, Blair Castle, Dumfries & Galloway Tourist Board, Alan Stout, Rod Wheelans, Inveraray Church and Bell-tower, Highlands and Islands Development Board Photographic Library, Museum of Childhood, Inverness Museum & Art Gallery, Inveraray Castle, Jarrold Publishing, The Pilgrim Press Ltd, Scone Palace, Royal Lochnagar Distillery, Nature Conservancy Council North West Region Scotland, Glenturret Distillery, Storybook Glen, The Royal Museum of Scotland, RSPB, The People's Story Museum, Matthew Cloag & Son Ltd, Charles Tait Photographic Orkney, The Palace of Holyroodhouse, Duthie Park Winter Gardens, William Grant & Sons Ltd.

INTRODUCTION

Scotland is a wonderful place. A sweeping
statement, indeed, but a true one. Scotland offers
the visitor, not only a hundred thousand welcomes,
but almost as many attractions. In this sturdy,
pocket-sized book, I have set out to give readers an
insight into my native country by writing 'sketches'
of little over a hundred of them. Selecting them has
been a painstaking and difficult task, but I decided
to concentrate on places for the discerning tourist –
culture-orientated places; places where nature is
treated leniently; places crammed with history and
folklore and places of scenic beauty: castles,
abbeys, churches, historic houses, museums and art
galleries, nature reserves, battlefields and
monuments. I have deliberately avoided bingo-
halls, places with Space Invaders, leisure complexes
and zoos.

From Shetland to Gretna Green and from St
Kilda to St Abb's Head, Scotland has an
embarrassment of riches. The scenery varies from
the towering, age-old peaks of the Highlands to the
flat coastal plains of the Solway and the Galloway
pasture-lands criss-crossed by dykes. Cliché or not,
visitors are spoiled for choice.

Many travellers visit Scotland for its historic
castles. They have much to say about Edinburgh
Castle, which must be the world's most famous, and
is certainly the most-visited in Scotland. I have
looked at the 'Pink Palace' of Drumlanrig; the
Queen Mother's childhood home of Glamis (the
most haunted castle in Britain); Cawdor, where
Shakespeare is said to have staged *Macbeth* – and
many other fortresses and palaces ranging in age
from Urquhart and Caerlaverock to Queen
Victoria's pile at Balmoral.

The four great Border abbeys are sketched here,
as are the two 'cradles of Christianity', Whithorn

and Iona. I have written about ten gardens, which range in style from formal Pitmedden to Scotland's southernmost garden, Logan Botanic Garden, which is brimming with rare, tropical plants.

You will read of Traquair, Scotland's oldest inhabited house, which lures visitors with its proprietary ale; and of Scone Palace, on whose site many monarchs were crowned. Take a wander, too, around Burns's Ellisland and Scott's Abbotsford.

I call in at a clutch of museums and art galleries, including the world-famous Burrell Collection, and – also in Glasgow – the more earthy People's Palace. I visit Loch Ness and talk about its famous monster, or alleged monster – for no evidence has come to light yet to prove its existence, though not for the want of trying.

The book deals with Scapa Flow, where so many servicemen lost their lives during the wars; Skara Brae with its remarkable prehistoric remains and Inveraray Bell-Tower, whose bells are of international renown.

The guide will tell you about natterjack toads, puffins, fulmars and kittiwakes; about Wallace, Bruce, Mary Queen of Scots, Livingstone and the man now known as Bonnie Prince Charlie. It tells of the panoramic views from Goat Fell and Glencoe, and relates the gory battles fought on Scottish soil: Killiecrankie, Bannockburn, Culloden and the massacre of Glencoe.

The Scottish Visitors' Almanac does not purport to be a definitive guide to the many tourist attractions of Scotland, but if it succeeds in enticing visitors to probe further, it will have achieved the author's objective.

THE CASTLES OF SCOTLAND

Scotland has the rare advantage of possessing a plethora of castles, which testify to the days when wars raged with the English. Each has its own distinctive character and style; some, like unique Caerlaverock and imposing Urquhart, are in ruins; others, such as Blair and Inveraray, are still home to clan chiefs; many, like Drumlanrig and Culzean, are packed with priceless works of art. Crathes is not alone in having a remarkable garden, and Drumlanrig, Brodick and Culzean are among those with excellent visitor centres, country parks and woodland walks.

Scottish castles are not just piles of rock; many have ghostly legends, and all are rich in history.

Property	**BALMORAL**
Location	A93, 8 m W of Ballater, Grampian
Age	19th century
Status	HM The Queen
Open	1 May–31 July, Mon–Sat *only* 1000–1700
Admission	Nominal charge, reduced rates for senior citizens, children free
Phone	03397 42334/5

Balmoral Castle is set in a beautiful forested area of Deeside which Queen Victoria called 'My dear paradise' in her *Journal of my life in the Highlands*.

Queen Victoria and Prince Albert rented the original castle in 1848 and bought the estate four years later, when they rebuilt the castle.

The grounds, gardens, an exhibition of works of art and paintings in the Castle Ballroom and a carriage exhibition are open to the public, between the dates shown above, each year.

Facilities include a refreshment room, country walks, pony trekking, pony cart rides – when ponies are available – and gift shops. Parking is available in the Grampian Regional Council car park, enquiries should be made at the Main Gate for facilities for the disabled.

From the public access donations are made to various charities.

Property	**BLAIR CASTLE**
Location	Blair Atholl 6 m NNW of Pitlochry, Tayside
Age	13th–19th centuries
Status	Duke of Atholl
Open	Apr–Oct, 1000–1800, except Apr, May, Oct, Sun 1400–1800 Last admission 1700
Admission	Nominal charge, reduced rates for children & senior citizens
Phone	079 681 207

This white-turreted baronial castle described by Queen Victoria as 'a large, white painted building' is the home of the Duke of Atholl, chief of the clan Murray, who is the only British subject allowed to maintain a private army – the Atholl Highlanders.

The oldest part of the castle, Cummings Tower, dates back to 1269.

The castle has played host to Mary, Queen of Scots, Prince Charles Edward Stuart and Victoria.

It has a splendid collection of furniture, portraits, armour and china. There are Jacobite relics and Masonic regalia; an arboretum established by the second Duke in the 1740s.

Facilities include a deer park, nature trails, caravan park, pony trekking, picnic area, licensed restaurant and shop. There is partial wheelchair access, and a toilet for disabled people.

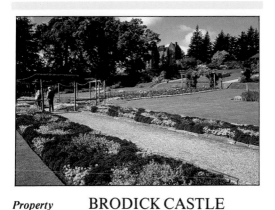

Property	**BRODICK CASTLE**
Location	Brodick, Isle of Arran, Strathclyde
Age	13th–19th centuries
Status	National Trust for Scotland (NTS)
Open	Castle: Apr–Sep, 1300–1700; Oct, Mon, Wed, Sat, 1300–1700 Garden and country park: all year 0930 to sunset
Admission	Nominal charge, reduced rate for children, less for gardens only, free car park
Phone	0770 2202

The ancient seat of the Dukes of Hamilton, Brodick Castle stands in the island's capital with a Wagnerian backdrop of bens and woodlands. It dates in part from the 13th century, but there were extensions built in 1652 and in 1844. The castle has a fine collection of Victorian sporting trophies and paintings, which are said to be Scotland's finest, and paintings from the collections of the Dukes of Hamilton, William Beckford and the Earls of Rochford.

The woodland garden, begun in 1923, is considered Europe's finest for rhododendrons, and the formal garden dating from 1710 has developed as a rose garden.

Facilities include a visitor centre, a ranger service, nature trail for wheelchair users, tea-room, shop, woodland walks and an adventure playground.

Property	**CAERLAVEROCK CASTLE**
Location	B725, 9 m S of Dumfries, Dumfries and Galloway
Age	13th century
Status	Scottish Development Department (SDD)
Open	Apr–Sep, 0930–1900, Sun 1400–1900 Oct–Mar, 0930–1600, Sun 1400–1600
Admission	Nominal charge, reduced rate for children & senior citizens
Phone	0387 77244

One of the finest castles in Scotland, Caerlaverock was the stronghold of the Wardens of the Western Marches, and the seat of the Maxwell family. It dates back to 1270 and is of a triangular layout unique in Britain.

Moated Caerlaverock has a chequered history: in 1297 Wallace rested here before routing the English; in 1300 it was besieged and captured by Edward I. The Covenanters laid siege in 1640 and Cromwell took it in 1651. It was occupied by Henry VIII and James V stayed in the castle before his defeat at the battle of Solway Moss in 1542. It fell into disrepair in the 1660s.

Caerlaverock's most notable features are a twin-towered gatehouse and the Nithsdale lodging, a splendid Renaissance range dating from 1638.

No visitor centre, refreshments or ranger service. Wheelchair access difficult.

Property	# CAWDOR CASTLE
Location	B9090, 5 m SW of Nairn, Highland
Age	14th century
Status	Earl of Cawdor
Open	May–Oct, 1000–1700
Admission	Nominal charge, reduced rates for disabled and senior citizens, less for grounds only
Phone	066 77 615

Cawdor Castle is famous as one of the settings for Shakespeare's *Macbeth*, and Duncan is said to have been murdered here (Shakespeare's *Macbeth* was the Thane of Cawdor).

The castle is equally noted for the thorn tree, which is dated 1372 and stands in what used to be the dungeon. Tradition has it that one of the Cawdor thanes had a dream, in which he was told to load a donkey with gold and make it wander at random. He would have to build his castle on the spot where the animal came to rest. It settled beside the thorn tree, and the master built around it.

The oldest part of the castle is the 14th-century central tower, fortified in 1454 and surrounded by 16th-century annexes.

The gardens are beautiful with extensive nature trails, a nine-hole pitch and putt course and a putting green. There is a licensed restaurant, a snack bar and picnic area, together with partial wheelchair access to castle, and toilets.

Property	# CRATHES CASTLE AND GARDEN
Location	A93, 3 m E of Banchory, Grampian
Age	16th century
Status	NTS
Open	Castle: Apr–Oct, 1100–1800 Gardens and Grounds: All year, 0930 to sunset
Admission 1991	Nominal charge, reduced rate for children, less for grounds only
Phone	033 044 525

Crathes, allegedly haunted by the Green Lady, was the home of the Burnetts for over 350 years and is one of the best preserved 16th-century castles in the country. It sits on a south-facing slope in pleasantly wooded countryside. It was built as a tower-house starting in 1553 and around 1599 the ceilings of the Chamber of the Nine Nobles, the Chamber of the Nine Muses and the Green Lady's Room were painted.

The Queen Anne and Victorian wings were destroyed by fire in 1966 and only the former was partially rebuilt. A four-acre walled garden includes a vast range of plants and shrubs, a croquet lawn and yew hedges (with topiary) which were planted in 1702. The 595-acre estate is rich in wildlife and has nature trails.

Facilities include a visitor centre with exhibitions, shop, licensed restaurant (recognised by 'Taste of Scotland'), plant sales centre, partial wheelchair access to castle, plus toilets for disabled people.

Property	**CULZEAN CASTLE**
Location	A719, 12 m SSW of Ayr, Strathclyde
Age	Built 1772–1792
Status	NTS
Open	Castle: 11–30 Apr, 1 Sep–31 Oct, 1200–1700 1–10 Apr, 1 May–31 Aug, 1000–1800 Park: all year round, 0900 to sunset
Admission	Nominal charge, reduced rate for children, grounds by donation
Phone	065 56 269

Cliff-top Culzean, the former seat of the Earls of Cassilis, is the Trust's flagship and is one of Robert Adam's most remarkable commissions. It has been described as 'a supremely important landmark in the history of Scotland'.

The castle's notable features include a magnificent oval staircase and round drawing-room. The Eisenhower Room traces the general's career and association with Culzean.

The castle's 565 acres of grounds, which became the first country park in Scotland, afford superb views across the Firth of Clyde to Arran and Ailsa Craig. The grounds have some 50 stone buildings, many of which are of international importance. There is also a gazebo, a pagoda, a dolphin tower, a ruined viaduct.

There is a ranger service and guided walks.

Other facilities include an adventure playground, talks and films with an induction loop, toilets for handicapped and disabled people and a restaurant.

Property	# DRUMLANRIG CASTLE
Location	A76, 3 m N of Thornhill, Dumfries and Galloway
Age	Late 17th century
Status	Duke of Buccleuch
Open	Apr–Aug (except Thurs) 1100–1700, Sun 1400–1800 Park: Apr–Sep 1100–1800, Sun 1400–1800
Admission	Nominal charge, reduced rates for children, students & senior citizens, less for grounds only
Phone	0848 30248/31555

Drumlanrig, the 'Pink Palace', is the Dumfriesshire home of the Duke of Buccleuch – a unique example of late 17th-century Renaissance architecture in sandstone, built in the site of an ancient stronghold of the Douglases.

The castle houses an internationally famous collection of art treasures, which includes works by Rembrandt, Gainsborough and Holbein – and a Madonna thought to be the only one by Leonardo da Vinci in a private collection.

The drawing-room has a cabinet presented by Louis XVI to Charles II, and the front hall has a tapestry believed to be the work of Mary, Queen of Scots.

There is a ranger service, restaurant, visitor centre, wheelchair access, adventure woodland, crafts centre.

Property	**EDINBURGH CASTLE**
Location	Castle Rock, Royal Mile, Edinburgh, Lothian
Age	Oldest 12th century
Status	SDD
Open	Apr–Sep, 0930–1705, Sun 1100–1705 Oct–Mar, 0930–1620, Sun 1230–1535
Admission	Nominal charge, reduced rates for children, senior citizens & families
Phone	031 225 9846

This castle is probably the world's most famous, and is visited by over a million people every year. It stands in the centre of the Scottish capital upon a volcanic plug, which has acted as a fortress point from ancient times. The earliest evidence of occupation of the rock is in the 6th century, but a castle did not exist until the 11th century.

The oldest building in the castle is a 12th-century chapel dedicated to St Margaret, who died in the castle shortly after hearing of the death of her husband, Malcolm III, and their eldest son. The fortress was repeatedly captured by the English during the 13th century, and David II undertook a major rebuilding programme during the 14th century.

The royal accommodation was crowned by the Great Hall built by James IV in the early 16th century, and Mary, Queen of Scots gave birth to James VI at the castle.

Edinburgh Castle became, to a large extent, the seat of government, and its military significance began to outweigh its function as a royal residence.

A half-moon battery was built by the Regent Morton in the late 16th century. In 1640 General Leslie besieged the castle, and Cromwell's troops took it ten years later. The Duke of Gordon unsuccessfully defend the castle against the forces of William and Mary in 1689, and in 1715 the Jacobites tried to capture the castle for the Old Pretender. During the 1745 rebellion, Prince Charles's troops tried again in vain to take it.

Restoration began in the 19th century with the support of Sir Walter Scott. His name was on a Royal Warrant to break open an oak chest in the Crown Room, which was thought to house the missing Crown Jewels. The jewels (Honours) are on display to this day. Another attraction is the famous 15th-century cannon, Mons Meg.

The Scottish National War Memorial was erected at the castle in the 1920s, and since 1947 the castle has been famous the world over as the venue of the annual military tattoo held on the Esplanade. It is also the headquarters for the Lowlands and Scottish Division, the Royal Scots and the Royal Scots Dragoon Guards. It also has the only army school of piping in the country.

The Scottish United Services Museum is housed within the castle. Exhibitions include 'Musket, Fife and Drum – 300 Years of British Military Music' and 'The Story of the Scottish Soldier'.

Facilities include partial wheelchair access, toilets for disabled people and a shop.

Property	**GLAMIS CASTLE**
Location	A928, 1 m N of Glamis, Tayside
Age	15th century
Status	Earl of Strathmore and Kinghorne
Open	Easter, May–Oct, daily 1200–1730, Jul–Aug from 1100
Admission	Nominal charge, reduced rates for children & senior citizens
Phone	030 784 242

Glamis, the childhood home of the Queen Mother, has the grisly reputation of being Scotland's most haunted castle. The Grey Lady is reputed to haunt the chapel, the devil himself is said to play cards in the sealed chamber of the crypt, and a little black page boy has seemingly been seen outside the Queen Mother's sitting-room. Tradition has it that Malcolm II was murdered on the site of the original castle in 1034, but the oldest surviving part is Duncan's Hall, the legendary setting of Shakespeare's *Macbeth* (*see* Cawdor Castle).

The castle, from which the Grampian mountains are visible, is set in magnificent parkland with an avenue of trees dating back to 1820. A two-acre Italian garden enclosed by yew hedges boasts an enormous 17th-century sundial with 84 dials, and statues of Charles I and James I. There is a substantial collection of china, paintings, tapestry and furniture.

Facilites include a self-service restaurant, gift shop, gallery, garden produce stall. Limited wheelchair access.

Property	## INVERARAY CASTLE
Location	0.5 m N of Inveraray, A83, Strathclyde.
Age	18th century
Status	Argyll Estates
Open	Apr–Jun, Sep–mid Oct, Mon–Sat (not Fri) 1000–1230, 1400–1700, Sun 1300–1730
Admission	Nominal charge, reduced rates for children & senior citizens
Phone	0499 2203

Inveraray Castle has been the seat of the Dukes of Argyll, chiefs of the clan Campbell, for centuries. It is a fairy-tale sort of castle: a pseudo-French chateau with gardens overlooking Loch Fyne and the Cowal hills.

The castle has many interesting historical relics including the nightcap worn by the Marquis of Argyll on the scaffold, muskets used at Culloden, German silver-gilt galleons on wheels, a set of Beauvais tapestries and a portrait of Lady Charlotte Campbell as Aurora, goddess of the dawn. There are portraits by Gainsborough, Ramsay and Raeburn.

A bronze cannon outside the entrance is said to have come from a Spanish Armada boat which was sunk in Tobermory Bay in 1588. The entrance itself was made of wrought iron and glass in order to protect Queen Victoria from the rain during her first visit.

There is a tea-room, a crafts shop, partial wheelchair access and a toilet for disabled people.

Property	**STIRLING CASTLE**
Location	Centre of Stirling, Central
Age	12th century
Status	SDD
Open	Apr–Sep, 0930–1715, Sun 1030–1645 Oct–Mar, 0930–1620, Sun 1230–1535
Admission	Nominal charge, reduced rates for children, senior citizens & families
Phone	0786 50000

Barring Edinburgh, Stirling Castle is Scotland's most prestigious fortress. Perched on a long-extinct volcano at 250 feet, it commands a strategic position on the Firth of Forth.

Both Robert the Bruce and William Wallace fought the English for the castle. Wallace re-captured it in 1297 while Bruce won it in 1314.

The castle became a royal residence, and James II of Scotland was born here in 1430. It was the childhood home of James IV, who built the old towers and the great hall. James V built the palace in a sumptuous Renaissance style from France. He also built mischievous facades on the palace which were condemned by the Victorian architect Robert Billings as 'abominations and obscene groups betraying the fruits of an imagination luxuriant but revolting'. Mary, Queen of Scots and James VI also lived here.

Notable features include the Chapel Royal of 1594, James V's palace and the 16th-century hall. There is a visitor centre with audio-visual display, a shop and tea-room.

Property	URQUHART CASTLE
Location	1.5 m SE of Drumnadrochit, Loch Ness, Highland
Age	13th century
Status	SDD
Open	Apr–Sep, 0930–1900, Sun 1400–1900 Oct–Mar, 0930–1600, Sun 1400–1600
Admission	Nominal charge, reduced rates for children & senior citizens
Phone	0456 2551

Urquhart Castle, though now in glorious ruins on the western shore of the alleged monster's loch, was once Scotland's largest castle. It was blown up in 1692 to prevent Jacobites taking possession.

James IV gifted the castle, which stood on the site of a vitrified fort, to John Grant of Freughie in 1509, and Grant's family renovated it.

The 16th-century tower is the best-preserved part of the castle, and there have been many 'sightings' of the legendary Loch Ness Monster from here.

SCOTLAND AT PRAYER

Scotland has a rich and turbulent religious heritage,
Christianity arrived in the fifth century AD, via
St Ninian, a Briton who converted the southern
Picts from paganism. He was based at Whithorn,
where important excavations are currently being
undertaken. St Columba did his share of the work
a century or so later from Iona. St Kentigern, St
Cuthbert and St Aidan were among the later
missionaries who contributed to the spread of
Christianity.

Many centuries later, great monastic houses were
formed, and many of the abbeys described here are
monuments to the spread of religion. The Historical
Buildings and Monuments Division of the Scottish
Development Department is to be congratulated on
the good work it does to preserve the past – against
the odds.

The four great Border abbeys, Melrose, Kelso,
Dryburgh and Jedburgh, suffered greatly at the
hands of the English, while the less accessible
Inchcolm Abbey and St Magnus Cathedral survived
in holy splendour.

St Orans Chapel, beside Iona Abbey

Property	**ARBROATH ABBEY**
Location	Arbroath, Tayside
Age	12th century
Status	SDD
Open	Summer 0930–1900, Sun 1400–1900 Winter 0930–1600, Sun 1400–1600
Admission	Nominal charge, reduced rates for children & senior citizens
Phone	0241 78756

This Tironensian abbey founded by William the Lion in 1178 is famous as the place where the Declaration of Arbroath was made on 6 April 1320 – declaring Robert the Bruce as king and asserting Scotland's independence from the English. The famous declaration by a group of Scottish barons was sent to Pope John XXII.

The abbey was dedicated to Thomas Becket and boasts one of the most outstanding examples of an abbot's house. Parts of the church and the domestic buildings remain.

Arbroath Abbey became the second richest religious house in Scotland (after Kelso), but it escaped the ravages of the English which plagued the great abbeys of the Borders. However, there were several outbreaks of fire here, and the abbey was attacked by reformers from Dundee.

Facilities include a visitor centre and easy access for wheelchairs. There is also a picnic area.

Property	**CRATHIE CHURCH**
Location	Crathie, 8 m W of Ballater, Grampian
Age	Built 1895
Status	Church of Scotland
Open	Apr–Oct 0930–1730, Sun 1400–1800 Sunday services 1130
Admission	Free
Phone	03397 42208

The uniqueness of Crathie Church is due to the close association Deeside has with the Royal Family. Since 1848, when Queen Victoria first visited the area, every British monarch has worshipped with the local congregation at Crathie on a Sunday.

The present church was built in 1895 to replace the building of 1804, and its foundation stone was laid in 1893 by the Queen. In style it is Gothic, although it has some Norman features. The tower houses four bells gifted by Queen Victoria's daughter, Princess Beatrice. The Royal Family has endowed the church with many other gifts, including an Iona marble communion table donated by George V in memory of Edward VII. Edward VII himself had gifted two white marble medallions in memory of the Duke of Saxe-Coburg and Gotha, and of Princess Victoria, Queen of Prussia. Queen Victoria presented a Father Willis organ, and our present Queen gifted a royal-crested Bible.

The south transept of the church is set apart for the Royal Family and household, while the north transept contains the pews of the lairds of Invercauld and Abergeldie

Property	**DRYBURGH ABBEY**
Location	Off A68, 6 m SE of Melrose, Borders
Age	12th century
Status	SDD
Open	Summer 0930–1900, Sun 1400–1900 Winter 0930–1600, Sun 1400–1600
Admission	Nominal charge
Phone	0835 22381

Dryburgh, one of the four great Border abbeys, stands on a picturesque site alongside the river Tweed near St Boswell's. It was the first Scottish home of the White Canons of the Premonstratensian order, and was founded in 1150 by Hugh Morville, Constable of David I.

The abbey was burned by the English in 1322, 1385, 1461 and 1523, but the ruins are remarkably complete. Much of the surviving building is dated as 12th–13th century.

Etched into a foundation stone in the ruined northern wall of the nave is a merelles board, merelles having been a board game, similar to the modern noughts and crosses, introduced into England by the Normans.

The abbey is most famous as the burial place of Scotland's most notable novelist, Sir Walter Scott. Field Marshal Earl Haig is also buried here. A huge statue of Sir William Wallace stands above the abbey.

Facilities include a visitor centre. Wheelchair access to the site is difficult.

Property	**DUNFERMLINE ABBEY**
Location	Pittencrieff Park, Dunfermline, Fife
Age	11th century
Status	SDD
Open	Summer 0930–1900, Sun 1400–1900
	Winter 0930–1600, Sun 1400–1600
Admission	Free
Phone	0383 739026

Dunfermline Abbey is the great Benedictine abbey founded by Queen Margaret, the wife of Malcolm Canmore, during the 11th century. The foundations of her church lie beneath the present remarkable Romanesque nave, which was consecrated in the 12th century. David I, who took an active interest in the spread of the abbeys, was St Margaret's son, and he brought an abbot from Canterbury in 1128 for the enlarged abbey.

Robert the Bruce was buried in the choir, which is now the site of the parish church. His grave is marked by a brass plaque in the choir. At the east end of the church are the remains of St Margaret's 13th century shrine. Next to the abbey is the ruin of the royal palace rebuilt from the monastery guest-house in the 16th century for James VI. Charles I, the last monarch born in Scotland, was born here.

The ruins of the abbey refectory and pend still remain. Facilities include two shops and partial wheelchair access.

Property	**DUNKELD CATHEDRAL**
Location	High Street, Dunkeld, near Perth, Tayside
Age	12th century
Status	SDD
Open	Summer 0930–1900, Sun 1400–1900 Winter 0930–1600, Sun 1400–1600
Admission	Free
Phone	0350 2601

Picturesquely situated on the banks of the River Tay, Dunkeld Cathedral is a haven of peace. It was founded in the 12th century on the site of an ancient church.

The refurbished choir is now used as the parish church, but the 15th-century nave and north-west tower are in the care of the Secretary of State for Scotland. The nave, restored in 1406, shows a Dutch influence – particularly the heavy cylindrical columns.

In 1689 Covenanting troops were trapped in the cathedral grounds, pinned down by Jacobites who were elated by their victory at Killiecrankie. The Covenanters rushed out with burning faggots attached to their halberds and set fire to thatched houses which sheltered Jacobite snipers. The National Trust for Scotland owns 20 houses near the cathedral, dating back to the rebuilding of the town after the battle.

Access to the cathedral for wheelchairs is difficult, and there is no visitor centre.

Property	**INCHCOLM ABBEY**
Location	Inchcolm Island, Firth of Forth, Fife
Age	13th century
Status	SDD
Open	Summer 0930–1900, Sun 1400–1900 Winter 0930–1600, Sun 1400–1600 Closed Thurs pm and Fri winter
Admission	Nominal charge, reduced rates for children & senior citizens
Phone	0383 823332

Inchcolm Abbey was founded in 1123 as an Augustinian church, but grew into an abbey in 1235. The remains are the best preserved group of monastic buildings in Scotland.

Inchcolm islet attracted many hermits, and the Danes paid through the nose to have their dead buried here a thousand years or so ago. Alexander I was storm-bound at Inchcolm in 1123, the year before he died, and the hermits gave him hospitality. It was he who set the plan for the abbey in motion.

This century Inchcolm was a strategic part of Scotland's defence network. It was garrisoned during the First World War, when the Forth estuary was one of the most heavily defended in the United Kingdom; and it was fortified with 500 men during the Second World War as a precaution against Hitler's invasion plans.

Ferries sail regularly to Inchcolm from South Queensferry and Aberdour.

Wheelchair access to the abbey is difficult. There are toilets and a picnic area.

Property	**INVERARAY BELL-TOWER**
Location	Inveraray, Argyll, Strathclyde
Age	20th century
Status	Scottish Episcopal Church of All Saints
Open	Summer 1000–1300, 1400–1700, Sun 1500–1800
Admission	Nominal charge, reduced rates for children & senior citizens, free exhibition
Phone	0499 2433

The bells! The bells! Campanologists take note: this 126-feet-high tower is world-famous. It contains Scotland's finest bells, which have the second heaviest ring of ten bells in the world (after Wells Cathedral).

Ringers may sometimes be seen (and heard) in action. At other times visitors have to be content with a recording of the unique sound.

The granite bell-tower is a memorial to the Campbells who fell in the First World War and was planned by the 10th Duke of Argyll in 1914. It had to wait until 1931 to open, and the Duke wrote a few years later: 'The belfry was gradually built to contain the fine peal of ten bells which are the finest north of the Tweed. Each bell bears the name of one of the old Celtic saints.'

Worth a visit for the views from the tower, and for the glorious sound of the bells ringing across loch and glen. There is partial wheelchair access.

Property	**IONA ABBEY**
Location	Island off coast of Mull, Strathclyde
Age	11th–13th century
Status	NTS (1897 acres of island), Abbey: private trust
Open	All reasonable times
Admission	By donation
Phone	068 17 404

Iona's prestige began in AD 563 when the Celtic bishop Columba and his 12 companions sailed from Ireland to found a monastery here. He used it as a base from which to convert the Picts to Christianity. The monastery was attacked and burned six times by Vikings and was eventually abandoned in favour of Kells in Ireland.

Iona was re-occupied in 1203 as a Benedictine monastery, but it fell into ruin during the Reformation when symbols of the Roman Catholic faith came under attack.

The oldest surviving building is St Oran's chapel (*c.* 1080), and the ornately carved St Martin's Cross (10th-century) stands outside the cathedral.

Today Iona is a sacred place visited by over 200,000 pilgrims per year. The Iona Community, founded by George MacLeod, now Lord MacLeod of Fuinary in 1938, has played a prominent part in the restoration of the abbey. Facilities include a book and gift shop, and a coffee-house.

The island is reached by ferry from Fionnphort or by steamer from Oban. No visitors' cars are allowed.

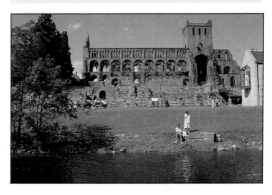

Property	**JEDBURGH ABBEY**
Location	High Street, Jedburgh, Borders
Age	12th century
Status	SDD
Open	Summer 0930–1900, Sun 1400–1900 Winter 0930–1600, Sun 1400–1600 Closed Oct–Mar Thurs pm and Fri
Admission	Nominal charge
Phone	0835 63925

This great Augustinian abbey founded by David I and
the Bishop of Glasgow around 1138 was burned nine
times by the marauding English and rebuilt eight times.
One of the first churches to be built in the more refined
Gothic style, in design it resembles a nunnery in
Hampshire where King David had lived. It has been
described as the most perfect and beautiful example of
the Saxon and early Gothic in Scotland.

Jedburgh Abbey's ruins are splendid and extensive.
They include a fine rose window on the west front
known as St Catherine's Wheel.

A new visitor centre at Jedburgh has displays and
models illustrating life in a medieval monastery and a
glazed gallery providing a magnificent view of the site.
A viewing route has been laid out through the abbey,
and the monks' herb garden has been re-planted.

There is limited wheelchair access, but there are
toilets for disabled people, and a shop.

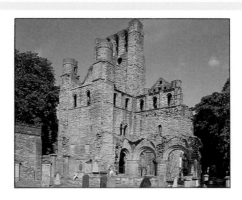

Property	**KELSO ABBEY**
Location	Bridge Street, Kelso, Borders
Age	12th century
Status	SDD
Open	Summer 0930–1900, Sun 1400–1900
	Winter 0930–1600, Sun 1400–1600
Admission	Free
Phone	No

Founded by David I in 1128 for the Tironensian order of monks, Kelso Abbey was the largest and wealthiest of the great Border abbeys. It was often attacked by the English, and the buildings were even evacuated for a while during the Wars of Independence.

In 1460 James III was crowned in the abbey and during the 16th century it was all but destroyed by the English. In 1545, the Earl of Hereford attacked the abbey, killed everybody in the garrison, including 12 monks, and burned it to the ground. The building was further mutilated during the Reformation, and is now in ruins. It is, none the less, an excellent piece of Romanesque architecture.

The abbey's design is unique in Scotland with both western and eastern transepts and a tower over both crossings. The Vatican archives still have a written description of the abbey in its heyday when it had 40 monks.

There are no visitor services, and wheelchair access is difficult.

Property	**MELROSE ABBEY**
Location	Main Square, Melrose, Borders
Age	12th–15th centuries
Status	SDD
Open	Summer 0930–1900, Sun 1400–1900 Winter 0930–1600, Sun 1400–1600
Admission	Nominal charge
Phone	0896 822 562

Melrose Abbey, Scotland's first Cistercian abbey, was founded by David I around 1136. It was repeatedly wrecked during the Wars of Independence, but most of its remains are of an elegance unique in Scotland – far finer than the usual Cistercian model. The ruin is probably Scotland's most famous, and most of the remains date back to the 15th century.

Richard II razed the abbey to the ground in 1385, and rebuilding was undertaken to a very ornate English design. Later a Parisian mason called John Morrow introduced more flamboyant stonework, including flying buttresses decorated with statuettes (on the roof there is a figure of a pig playing the bagpipes!).

Part of the nave was used as a parish church as late as the 19th century. Unusually for Scotland, the church is totally vaulted and the cloisters face north.

Melrose Abbey is famous as the burial-place of Robert the Bruce's heart, of Alexander II and of Michael Scott, the 13th-century philosopher who became known as 'the wizard of the North'.

There is a visitor centre with easy access for disabled people.

Property	**RUTHWELL CROSS**
Location	B724 8 m SE of Dumfries, Dumfries and Galloway
Age	7th century
Status	SDD
Open	All reasonable times
Admission	Free
Phone	No

The Ruthwell Cross is one of the most important attractions on the Solway Coast Heritage Trail. A runic cross, it dates back to about AD 680 and bears the oldest extant fragment of written English. The cross is a priceless work of art and is considered to be one of the major monuments of Dark Age Europe.

The cross was nearly destroyed as an 'idolatrous monument' during the Reformation. The General Assembly of the Church of Scotland ordered its destruction, but a succession of forward-thinking ministers of the parish craftily conserved it for posterity. One of them was the Revd Henry Duncan, who founded the world's first bona fide savings bank at Ruthwell.

The cross is 18 feet high and stands in the parish church. It was designed to tell the story of the Life and Passion of Christ – a sermon on stone. It bears figure sculptures and Latin inscriptions.

The key to the church can be obtained at Kirkyett cottage. There is wheelchair access to church with assistance

Property	**ST ANDREW'S CATHEDRAL**
Location	St Andrew's, Fife
Age	12th century
Status	SDD
Open	All hours Museum and tower, standard daily hours
Admission	Nominal charge
Phone	0334 72563

This magnificent cathedral founded in 1160 in one of Europe's major historical cities used to be the largest church in Scotland. Thousands of pilgrims travelled here to pray at the 31 altars. Sadly it is now in ruins.

The remains of the church dedicated to Scotland's patron saint include portions of the east and west gables, the south wall of the nave and parts of the choir and south transept. Some of the domestic ranges of the priory have also survived. The museum houses a wealth of fascinating relics including a unique sarcophagus dated around AD 900.

The cathedral was founded in 1160 as a replacement to the 12th-century Augustinian church of St Rule, and was consecrated in 1318. The precinct walls are the finest surviving examples in Scotland, and were built in 1520. Nearby are the remains of the square St Rule's Tower, which has a Northumbrian look about it.

There is wheelchair access to the ground floor and gardens.

Property	**ST MAGNUS CATHEDRAL**
Location	Kirkwall, Orkney
Age	12th century
Status	Local authority
Open	Mon–Sat 0900–1300, 1400–1700, Sun services
Admission	Free
Phone	0856 3535

St Magnus Cathedral is the only medieval Scottish cathedral to have survived intact, and has been described as 'the crown of the Northern Isles'. A noble monument to Scotland's heritage, it is a classic sight.

The cathedral, made of sandstone, was founded by the Norseman Jarl Rognvald in 1137 in memory of his uncle St Magnus, who had been murdered by a rival 20 years beforehand. The polychrome stonework – yellow and red – is said to be the best of its age in Britain.

St Magnus has a number of small commemorative plaques, too, including one in memory of the men who perished on HMS *Royal Oak* when it was sunk during the Second World War. Another bears the name of Edwin Muir, the poet.

The method of ringing the cathedral bells, known as 'clocking', has Norse links and is said to be unique in the United Kingdom.

Orkney's midsummer festival is also named after St Magnus.

Property	**WHITHORN PRIORY**
Location	Whithorn, 10 m S of Wigtown, Dumfries and Galloway
Age	12th century
Status	SDD
Open	Summer, daily 1030–1700
Admission	Dig, visitor centre: Nominal charge, reduced rates for children, unemployed & senior citizens Priory: Nominal charge, reduced rate for children
Phone	098 85 508

St Ninian built Scotland's first recorded Christian church at Whithorn during the fifth century – long before Columba reached the shores of Iona.

Archaeologists have been investigating the site since 1986 and have discovered some significant remains, including those of a Viking settlement. If visitors don't mind skeletons, they will enjoy the Whithorn Dig, which received a *Glasgow Herald* award in 1987 for the site offering the most to the public. Since then a visitor centre has opened.

During the Middle Ages St Ninian's shrine became one of Western Europe's most renowned seats of learning, and many monarchs made the pilgrimage – including Mary, Queen of Scots, Robert the Bruce, Queen Margaret of Denmark and James V.

The Dig Shop sells books, postcards and craft work. The visitor centre has audio-visual aids, and guided tours are available.

SCOTLAND'S HISTORIC HOMES

Scotland abounds with houses which echo with
history – from romantic 10th-century Traquair and
its associations with the Jacobite cause, to the royal
palaces of Holyrood, Falkland and Scone. Many a
fortnight's holiday could be planned around visits
to the countless important mansion houses. Every
region is studded with grand houses which, if they
could speak, would have many a tale to tell.

The cities also have their share of glory.
Edinburgh's New Town has a wealth of Georgian
architecture, Charlotte Square being the
masterpiece. The capital's Old Town is just as
thought-provoking. Gladstone's Land, for
instance, is a symbol of 17th-century urban
architecture. Way out west – in Glasgow – there is
Pollok House with its famous Burrell Collection of
arts and antiques, and Provand's Lordship, an
oddity from the Middle Ages.

Property	**FALKLAND PALACE**
Location	A912, 11 m N of Kirkcaldy
Age	16th century
Status	Crown/NTS
Open	Apr–Sep, 1000–1800, Sun 1400–1800 Oct, Sat 1000–1800, Sun 1400–1800
Admission	Nominal charge, reduced rate for children, less for gardens only Scots Guards free
Phone	033 757 397

This royal palace in the pretty Fife town of Falkland is of the Renaissance style and was built by James IV and James V between 1501 and 1541. A country residence of the Stewart kings, it was a favourite seat of James V, who died here in 1542. Mary, Queen of Scots spent the happiest days of her sad life here playing in the woods as a child, while her elders hunted deer and wild boar in the Fife forest.

The showpiece of the palace is the Chapel Royal in the roofed south range, and the east range contains the King's bedchamber, and the Queen's Room restored in 1987 to commemorate Mary, Queen of Scots.

In the beautiful gardens is an attractive lawn reflecting the 'lang butts' where James V practised archery. The tennis court for 'Real' or 'Royal' tennis, built in 1539, is the oldest in Britain, and is still used by the Falkland Real Tennis Club.

Facilities include a visitor centre, shop, picnic area and access for disabled people.

Property	**GEORGIAN HOUSE**
Location	7, Charlotte Square, Edinburgh, Lothian
Age	18th century
Status	NTS
Open	Apr–Oct, 1000–1700, Sun 1400–1700
Admission	Nominal charge, reduced rate for children
Phone	031 225 2160

Charlotte Square was built at the end of the 18th century and is acknowledged as a masterpiece of European urban architecture. It is the showpiece of Edinburgh's New Town, and the north side is partly the result of a design by Robert Adam, the leading architect of his time.

The square was built between 1792 and the early 19th century, and the lower floors of Georgian House were restored by the Trust and furnished as closely as possible to the late 18th century. It was opened in 1975 and is now a focal point for visitors to the New Town.

There is an audio-visual display, (with induction loops for those with hearing difficulties), reflecting the social conditions of the period. There are facilities for functions and a Trust shop. Induction loop for people with hearing difficulties.

Number 6, renamed Bute House, is the official residence of the Secretary of State for Scotland.

Property	**GLADSTONE'S LAND**
Location	477B, Lawnmarket, Royal Mile, Edinburgh, Lothian
Age	17th century
Status	NTS
Open	Apr–Oct, 1000–1700, Sun 1400–1700 Nov, Sat 1000–1630, Sun 1400–1630
Admission	Nominal charge, reduced rate for children & group rates
Phone	031 226 5856

Gladstone's Land, originally the home of Thomas Gledstones, a city burgess, is a typical example of an Old Town 17th-century tenement building. In fact, it is the best example in Edinburgh.

Gledstones rebuilt the house around 1620 in six storeys. He removed the timber galleries and built a stone-arcaded front which projected five yards or so into the street.

During the 1630s the building was home to five families. Particularly noteworthy are the splendid painted ceilings. The reconstructed shop booths exhibit replicas of 17th-century goods. The main rooms of the house have been refurbished as a typical period residence.

Facilities include a Trust shop and an induction loop for people with hearing difficulties.

Property	**PALACE OF HOLYROODHOUSE**
Location	Bottom of Royal Mile, Edinburgh, Lothian
Age	12th, 16th and 17th centuries
Status	Crown
Open	Apr–Oct, 0930–1715, Sun 1030–1630 Nov–Mar, 0930–1545 (not Sun) closed during Royal and state visits
Admission	Nominal charge, reduced rates for children & senior citizens
Phone	031 556 1096

Throughout history romantic Holyrood – which stands against the background of Salisbury Crags – has been the scene of the most turbulent and extraordinary events in Scottish history, the most dramatic of which was the murder of David Riccio, secretary to Mary, Queen of Scots.

Queen Mary met John Knox here and Prince Charles Edward Stuart held court in 1745. Charles I visited Holyrood twice and Charles II was crowned here.

The bedchamber where Riccio was murdered had been rebuilt by James V in 1529 and is preserved in the tower residence.

George V and later Queen Elizabeth, the Queen Mother, stayed at Holyrood regularly, as does the present Royal Family.

Facilities include a tea-room, wheelchair access on prior application, and a shop.

Property	**HOUSE OF DUN**
Location	A935 3 m W of Montrose, Tayside
Age	Early 18th century
Status	NTS
Open	Gardens: all year, 0930–sunset House and courtyard: Apr–Oct, 1100–1730
Admission	Nominal charge, reduced rate for children
Phone	067 481 264

The House of Dun is a Palladian house overlooking the
Montrose basin, and built in 1730 by Donald Erskine,
Lord Dun, to a William Adam design.

The Trust re-opened the building in 1989 after a £1
million restoration programme. An archway remains
of the old 15th-century castle of Dun.

Augusta Clarence, the illegitimate daughter of
William IV and the actress Mrs Jordan, renovated the
house with her husband, John Erskine Kennedy-
Erskine. It later became a hotel.

The Trust has refurbished the house in early-
Georgian and late-Regency decor. The courtyard
buildings house a visitor centre and a tea-room called
Lady Augusta's Kitchen.

There are woodland walks and trails, as well as a
picnic area. Other facilities include toilets for disabled
people and braille sheets for the blind and partially-
sighted.

Property	**POLLOK HOUSE**
Location	Pollokshaws Road, Glasgow, Strathclyde
Age	18th century
Status	Glasgow Museums and Art Galleries
Open	1000–1700, Sun 1400–1700
Admission	Free
Phone	041 632 0274

Three miles from the city centre stands the ancestral home of the Maxwells, which was bequeathed to the City of Glasgow in 1966 along with its 361 acres of rolling parklands and gardens.

The central block of the house is Glasgow's most significant surviving piece of 18th-century domestic architecture. It is of the neo-Palladian style. Additional wings were built at the turn of the century.

Inside is one of the finest group of Spanish paintings in Britain – including works by El Greco, Goya and Murillo. Other European masters represented include Blake, Mengs and Signorelli.

The furniture is from 1750 to 1820, and there are displays of high quality silver, ceramics and glass.

The adjacent country park is Glasgow's largest and finest park – a wildlife haven in an urban setting.

Other attractions include the world-famous Burrell Collection (see separate entry); a herd of pedigree Highland cattle, a demonstration garden and a woodland garden.

There is partial wheelchair access, a ranger service, a tea-room and a shop.

Property	**PROVAND'S LORDSHIP**
Location	3, Castle Street, Glasgow, Strathclyde
Age	15th century
Status	Glasgow Museums and Art Galleries
Open	1000–1700, Sun 1400–1700
Admission	Free
Phone	041 552 8819

Provand's Lordship is Glasgow's oldest house and the only surviving medieval building in the city apart from the cathedral – which it faces.

Bishop Andrew Muirhead built the house in 1471 as a manse for St Nicholas Hospital and the cathedral. It was the country house of the prebendary of Barlanark.

Provand's Lordship has a fascinating history. Mary, Queen of Scots is supposed to have stayed here, and last century it was used as a tavern – with the city executioner staying next door. It has also been a confectioner's shop, and the sweet-making machines are still on display.

The building has been greatly altered over the years, and many of the windows are from the 18th century. The back of the house, with three crow-stepped gables, is the nearest to the original building.

Nowadays the house has a splendid collection of 17th-century Scottish furniture and there are period displays, including stained-glass panelling.

There is partial access for disabled people, a sales area and car park.

Property	**PROVOST SKENE'S HOUSE**
Location	Broad Street, Aberdeen, Grampian
Age	16th century
Status	Local authority
Open	1000–1700, not Sun
Admission	Free
Phone	0224 641086

This attractive town mansion is an excellent example of traditional 17th-century Scottish domestic architecture, although the original building was erected in 1545. It is named after Sir George Skene, a wealthy merchant who was Provost of Aberdeen from 1676 until 1685.

In 1746 the house was commandeered by the Duke of Cumberland, a scourge of the Jacobites, and in more recent years it was a lodging-house.

Restoration work began in 1951 and each room is now endowed with interesting relics and period decor and furniture. The painted ceilings are outstanding, and there are displays of local history and a videotape giving an introduction to the house.

The top floor houses a museum of civic and domestic history.

Property	**SCONE PALACE**
Location	A93, 2 m NE of Perth, Tayside
Age	19th century
Status	Earl of Mansfield
Open	Easter–Oct, 0930–1700, Sun 1330–1700 July and Aug, 1000–1700
Admission	Nominal charge, reduced rates for children & senior citizens, less for grounds only
Phone	0738 52300

Scone Palace is awash with history. Although the present building was erected in 1803, the site was the seat of government from Pictish times onwards, and the crowning place of Scottish kings, including Macbeth and Robert the Bruce. The last coronation in Scotland – that of Charles II – took place here on Moat Hill in 1651.

Scone was enlarged and embellished in 1802 by the third Earl of Mansfield, although it incorporates a 16th-century building. The palace houses a splendid collection of ivories, French furniture, clocks and 16th-century needleworks, including bed-hangings by Mary, Queen of Scots. It has one of the finest collections of porcelain in Scotland.

Scone also possesses a famous pinetum containing rare pines. There are pleasant walks through the grounds, a restaurant, a shop and access for disabled people.

Property	**TRAQUAIR HOUSE**
Location	Innerleithen, B707 nr Peebles, Borders
Age	10th century
Status	P. Maxwell-Stuart
Open	Summer, 1330–1730 (July, Aug, first two weeks Sep, 1030–1730)
Admission	Nominal charge, reduced rate for children
Phone	0896 830323

Romantic Traquair in the Borders has the distinction of being Scotland's oldest continuously inhabited house, and is a thousand years old. Twenty-seven monarchs have stayed here and Alexander I signed a charter here 800 years ago.

Traquair's famous Bear Gates have been kept closed since 1745, the year Prince Charles Edward Stuart stayed here, and they will not be re-opened until a Stuart ascends the throne.

Another offbeat (but refreshing) feature of the mansion house is its home brew. An 18th-century brewery here produces up to 60,000 bottles of beer a year, most of them for export.

The grounds have a maze, a croquet lawn and woodland walks beside the River Tweed. There is a restaurant, a gift shop, craft workshops and an art gallery. Other facilities include partial access for disabled people, and special toilets.

SCOTLAND AT WAR

Colourful clan gatherings, famous Scottish regiments and the many folk ballads and pipers' tunes of glory are all reminders of Scotland's dabblings in warfare and strife. Scotland's countryside, moreover, bristles with memorials to the Covenanters who martyred themselves during the 'Killing Times', and with monuments to the Jacobite struggles. Plenty of evidence survives, too, of the resistance by Bruce, Wallace *et al* against English domination.

Every 'son of Donald' knows about Glencoe, and people with Jacobite sentiments still lament Culloden. In more modern times, Scapa Flow was an important naval base during the last war, and the scene during the First World War of the Germany navy's mass 'scuttle'.

Property	**BANNOCKBURN**
Location	2 m S of Stirling, Central
Historical Period	14th century
Status	NTS
Open	Heritage centre/shop: Apr–Oct 1000–1800
Admission	Nominal charge, reduced rate for children
Phone	0786 812664

Bannockburn is a name that has been on the lips of generations of Scottish schoolchildren. The name represents Scotland's most important victory over the English – in 1314. The battlefield, where Robert the Bruce routed the forces of Edward II and won freedom for the Scottish people, is one of the most important historic sites in Britain.

Bannockburn Heritage Centre stands a few yards from the famous Borestone site, the reputed location of Bruce's command-post. It is enclosed by the rotunda focusing on the approach route of the English army to Stirling Castle. The rotunda was opened by the Queen in 1964, when she unveiled a statue to Scotland's most celebrated king.

The centre displays an exhibition relating the story of the battle in three languages, and an exhibition entitled The Kingdom of the Scots.

Facilities include a tea-room and restaurant, a sales area and access for wheelchairs.

Property	BRUCE'S STONES
Location	6 m W of New Galloway, and N side of Loch Trool, Dumfries and Galloway
Historical Period	14th century
Status	NTS and private
Open	All year round
Admission	Free
Phone	No

The stone at the entrance to Glen Trool, three miles north of Newton Stewart, is a massive granite reminder of Robert the Bruce's first victory over the English in March 1307 in the run-up to Bannockburn. It commands a fine view of Loch Trool and the Galloway Hills, and is the traditional starting-point for the gruelling jaunt up Merrick, at 2764 feet the highest mountain in southern Scotland.

The stone on Moss Raploch by the A712 is in the care of the National Trust for Scotland, and marks the spot where Bruce defeated the English forces in his initial drive towards Scottish independence.

Property	**CULLODEN**
Location	5 m E of Inverness, Highland
Historical Period	18th century
Status	NTS
Open	All year round Visitor centre: Apr–May, Sep–Oct 0930–1730 Jun–Sep, 0900–1830
Admission	Centre: Nominal charge, reduced rate for children
Phone	0463 790607

Culloden was the scene of the last major battle on mainland Britain – which ended with the Stuart dreams of regaining the throne. On 16 April 1746, Prince Charles Edward Stuart and his Jacobite army were trounced by government forces led by the Duke of Cumberland – within 40 minutes of fighting.

Troops fought on moorland around Old Leanach Cottage, which survived the fray and has been refurbished with period furnishings.

Visitors to Culloden can view several memorials. The visitor centre has a colourful historical display and an audio-visual programme in six languages (English, French, Gaelic, German, Italian and Japanese). There is an auditorium, study room bookshop and self-service restaurant. There are toilets for disabled people, and an induction loop for people with hearing difficulties. A wheelchair is also available.

Property	**GLENCOE**
Location	A82, Lochaber, Highland
Historical Period	17th century
Status	NTS
Open	Information Centre: 1 Apr–25 May and 10 Sep–21 Oct, 1000–1730 26 May–9 Sep, 0930–1830
Admission	Nominal charge, reduced rate for children, including parking
Phone	085 52 307

Mention Glencoe in the right company and it sends a shiver down the spine or glazes the eyes. The awe-inspiring glen is as well known as Gretna Green and the Loch Ness Monster; in fact it is known the world over as the site where the Campbells massacred the MacDonalds in 1692.

A slim Celtic cross commemorates MacIain, Chief of Glencoe, who fell with his people in the massacre, which was the result of clan rivalry, and of the unwillingness of MacIain, chief of the MacDonalds, to sign an oath of allegiance to William of Orange in return for a pardon. MacIain wrote to the exiled King James VII for permission to take the oath. He received it, but left his submission at Inveraray to the last minute, and eventually took the oath five days after the deadline of New Year's Day, 1692.

Sir John Dalrymple, the Secretary of State, ordered

the clan MacDonald to be exterminated. Captain
Robert Campbell of Glenlyon did his dirty work for
him. He led the Argyll army into the glen on 1 February
and asked MacIain for hospitality. This he got, but 12
days later the slaughter began. MacIain was shot in the
back as he got out of bed; his wife was beaten to death;
and children and old folk were butchered. Many
escaped, but most of those died in the cold.

Glencoe, however, is not all blood and guts; it is the
spiritual home of many a mountaineer and hill-walker.
Although Dickens called it 'perfectly terrible . . . an
awful place . . . scores of glens high up, which form
such haunts as you might imagine yourself wandering
in, the very height and madness of a fever', it provides
some of the finest climbing and walking terrain in
Scotland. In 1976 The Leishman Memorial Centre, a
laboratory for research into mountain safety, was
opened at Achnacon on land bought from the Forestry
Commission.

The Trust now owns 14,200 acres of Glencoe. One of
the attractions is Ossian's Cave, associated with the
legends of the ancient Scottish bard. It is accessible by
climbing 200 feet on the face of Aonach Dubh, the
shoulder of Bidean nam Bian.

Facilities include a ranger service, an information
centre, a snack bar, Trust shop, exhibitions, picnic
area, and facilities for disabled people.

Property	**GLENFINNAN**
Location	A830, 18 m W of Fort William, Highland
Historical Period	18th century
Status	NTS
Open	All year. Centre: 1 Apr–25 May and 10 Sep–21 Oct, 1000–1300, 1400–1730 26 May–9 Sep, 0930–1830
Admission	Nominal charge, reduced rate for children
Phone	039 783 250

This monument, set in spectacular Highland scenery at the head of Loch Shiel, commemorates the raising of Prince Charles Edward Stuart's standard on 19 August 1745. It was his last-ditch attempt to put a Stuart back on the throne of the United Kingdom.

The monument was erected by Alexander Macdonald of Glenaladale in 1815 in tribute to the Highlanders who died in the Jacobite cause. The figure of a clansman stands on top of the famous tower.

In the visitor centre there are displays (with commentary in four languages) of the Prince's campaign from Glenfinnan to Culloden. The annual Glenfinnan Games take place in August.

Facilities at Culloden include a snack bar, a shop and access for wheelchairs.

Property	**KILLIECRANKIE**
Location	A9, 3 m N of Pitlochry, Tayside
Historical Period	17th century
Status	NTS
Open	Centre: 1 Apr–31 May, 1 Sep–28 Oct, 1000–1700 1 Jun–31 Aug, 0930–1800
Admission	Nominal charge, reduced rate for children
Phone	0796 3233

If Culloden marked the end of the Jacobite cause, Killiecrankie was the beginning. The battle took place at a wooded gorge a mile from Trust property in 1689 and government troops led by King William were routed. The Jacobite forces were led by John Graham of Claverhouse, who was mortally wounded in battle. He is forever rememberd in the popular song, 'Bonnie Dundee'.

One government soldier fleeing from battle made a spectacular leap across the river worthy of a long-jump champion. The place is now known as Soldiers Leap.

The wooded gorge was one of Queen Victoria's favourite spots, and there are numerous interesting walks. The pass is on the network of Garry-Tummel walks, which cover a distance of 20 miles.

The visitor centre features the battle and the natural history of the area. There is a ranger service, a shop and snack bar, as well as access for disabled people.

Property	## SCAPA FLOW VISITOR CENTRE
Location	The Pumphouse, Lyness, Orkney
Historical Period	20th century
Status	Local authority
Open	Mon–Fri 0915–1600; Sat 0915–1700; Sun 0930–1630
Admission	Nominal charge
Phone	0856 3535

Scapa Flow around Orkney was the scene of the surrender of the German Fleet in 1919, and a major naval anchorage in both world wars. The centre at Lyness, a wartime naval base, is a tribute to the army personnel who lost their lives there during the wars, and houses an extensive collection of wartime artefacts and memorabilia.

The Pumphouse itself was a hub of activity during the Second World War, when Scapa Flow was a 'Category A defended port'. Visitors can see the machinery which was used to heat and pump oil. Within the forecourt of the centre are several items which bear witness to the historic events around Orkney during the wars. There is a massive propellor from HMS *Hampshire*, which struck a mine off Birsay in 1916, with the loss of all but twelve of her crew. Among the victims was Lord Kitchener of Khartoum, the Minister for War.

SCOTLAND'S
CULTURAL HERITAGE

The designation of Glasgow as European City of Culture in 1990 was no accident. Despite its past reputation as an industrial centre, the city is bursting with art galleries and museums. And Glaswegians tell you that their home has more parks (66 in all) than any other city in Europe.

The Burrell Collection, opened in 1983, in Pollok Country Park, is an emblem of the city's cultural status: its composition and extent is quite bewildering – from prehistoric times to the Victorian era. Social history is the forte of the People's Palace on Glasgow Green, and it is told in a grass roots sort of a way. The Museum of Transport is a *must* for the train and tram enthusiasts.

Edinburgh's status as a cultural centre needs no introduction. Suffice to say that the famous Royal Mile is lined with interesting museums, among them the offbeat Museum of Childhood, which attracts hordes of adults as well as children.

Property	**ABERDEEN ART GALLERY AND MUSEUM**
Location	Schoolhill, Aberdeen, Grampian
Status	Local authority
Open	1000–1700, Sun 1400–1700, Thu 1000–2000
Admission	Free
Phone	0224 632133

The gallery houses one of the most important provincial art collections in the UK, ranging from 18th-century portraits by Raeburn, Hogarth, Ramsay and Reynolds to 20th-century works by Francis Bacon and Ben Nicholson. There are excellent examples by Impressionists such as Monet, Bonnard and Toulouse-Lautrec and work by E. A. Hornel, one of the 'Glasgow Boys'.

There are watercolours, sculptures and a significant collection of Scottish domestic silver, and glass from north-east Scotland.

The gallery presents a lively programme of special exhibitions. There is a reference library and a print room.

Built in 1885 to a neo-classical design, the building has a unique collection of 28 granite pillars in an Ionic style surrounding an Italianate courtyard. Extensions were made in later years.

Facilities include a coffee shop, sales area and ramped accessed throughout for wheelchairs.

Property	**BURRELL COLLECTION**
Location	Pollok Country Park, Glasgow, Strathclyde
Status	Local authority
Open	1000–1700, Sun 1400–1700
Admission	Free
Phone	041 649 7151

The award-winning museum is situated in beautiful parkland in the middle of Glasgow, and its collection boasts over 8000 artefacts ranging from textiles to furniture, ceramics, stained glass and *objets d'art* – all gifted to the city by Sir William Burrell, a shipping magnate, in 1944.

The exhibits cover an astonishing range from the ancient world to the 20th century. There are antiquities from Iraq, Egypt, Greece and Italy: Egyptian stone vases, Assyrian reliefs, Greek ceramics and Roman glassware.

The collection features Chinese ceramics dating from Neolithic times until last century, and they are complemented by jades and bronzes. There are Japanese prints, Eastern carpets and a comprehensive collection of North European decorative arts. The tapestries and stained glass work are world-famous.

Facilities include a restaurant, lecture theatre, room for children, library and study facilities and accommodation for scholars. There is ramped access to all facilities.

Property	**CITY ART CENTRE**
Location	2 Market Street, Edinburgh, Lothian
Status	Local authority
Open	Winter, 1000–1700, Mon–Sat Summer, 1000–1800
Admission	Free
Phone	031 225 2424

The capital city's permanent fine art collection is housed in this building opened in 1980 behind Waverley Station. The collection comprises over 3000 drawings, prints and sculptures from the 17th century to the present day, and there are regular exhibitions drawn from throughout Britain and overseas. An example in 1990 was The Art of Lego, a specially commissioned display of Lego works of art by artists, designers, architects, engineers and scientists. Others included an exhibition of funeral masks, ceremonial knives, necklaces and idols (and a mummified arm and hand) from Peru; and one on folk art from Nova Scotia, Canada.

The gallery's main strength lies in works by late-19th and 20th-century Scottish painters.

There is a licensed cafe, a shop and facilities for disabled people. Parties are welcome, but they ought to book.

Property	GLASGOW ART GALLERY AND MUSEUM
Location	Kelvingrove Park, Glasgow, Strathclyde
Status	Local authority
Open	1000–1700, Sun 1400–1700
Admission	Free
Phone	041 357 3929

This has been acknowledged as Britain's finest civic art collection. It opened in 1902 and includes works from all the major European schools. Categories include The Classical Tradition, The Art of the Church, The Realist Tradition and Art and Design, The Victorian Age and the Modern Period.

The collection has French painting of the Barbizon, Impressionist and Post-Impressionist periods, and there are examples of work by the 'Glasgow Boys' and the Scottish colourists.

The museum contains internationally important examples of European armour, Scottish and Egyptian archaeology, as well as a display of Scottish prehistoric artefacts. The natural history exhibition illustrates geology and dinosaurs; and there is a good collection on British birds.

The museum has a series of competitions and activities for juniors, including an annual young persons' art contest. There is access for disabled people, a refreshment area and a shop.

Property	**INVERNESS MUSEUM AND ART GALLERY**
Location	Castle Wynd, Inverness, Highland
Status	Local authority
Open	Weekdays 0900–1700
Admission	Free
Phone	0463 237114

This museum of the Highlands, established in 1881, covers social and natural history, archaeology and culture. It has an excellent collection of bagpipes and Jacobite relics. The lively 'Man in the Landscape' exhibition on the ground floor explores aspects of the environment in and around Inverness. Upstairs there is a mixture of weapons from the Highlands and Scottish contemporary art.

The gallery also boasts an important collection of Highland silver from Inverness, Tain and Wick dating from the mid-17th century until the present day. Local industry is portrayed in a reconstructed Inverness cottage of the 1930s and a taxidermist's workshop.

There is partial access for disabled people, and a toilet for those confined to wheelchairs. Other facilities include refreshments, a shop and temporary exhibitions.

Property	**MUSEUM OF CHILDHOOD**
Location	Royal Mile, Edinburgh, Lothian
Status	Local authority
Open	Mon–Sat 1000–1700; June–Sep, 1000–1800
Admission	Free
Phone	031 225 2424

This was the first museum in the world to be devoted solely to the history of childhood. A treasure-house of historic toys, dolls, dolls' houses, hobby items, children's costumes, nursery equipment and so on, it has been called the world's noisiest museum.

It was extended in 1986 into a former Georgian theatre, and completely renovated. Noteworthy exhibits include a pierrot serenading the moon, dated 1880; and a selection of Bisque dolls. There are also special areas devoted to children's games, and audio-visual and education rooms.

There is partial wheelchair access, plus a toilet for disabled people, and sales area.

Property	**MUSEUM OF TRANSPORT**
Location	Kelvin Hall, 1, Bunhouse Road, Glasgow, Strathclyde
Status	Local authority
Open	1000–1700, Sun 1400–1700
Admission	Free
Phone	041 357 3929

This mecca for transport enthusiasts mirrors sixty years of Glasgow trams and the glory-days of the River Clyde. The museum interprets the history of transport on land and sea, and the exhibits range from trains to buses, from trams to Scottish-built cars and from yachts to warships. There are horse-drawn vehicles, railway locomotives, fire engines, bicycles and motor cycles.

One of the star attractions is a simulated Glasgow street with 1938 shop facades and period vehicles parked on the cobbles. There is a reconstruction of Merkland Subway Station on the Glasgow Underground the third oldest underground network in the world. There is a showroom of cars through the ages, and the cycle display's centrepiece is the world's oldest pedal-bike, invented by Kirkpatrick Macmillan.

There are models of ships reflecting the golden age of shipping: ocean liners, paddle steamers and sailing ships.

Full facilities for disabled people are available, as well as a fast-food bar.

Property	**NATIONAL GALLERY OF SCOTLAND**
Location	The Mound, Edinburgh, Lothian
Status	Trustees
Open	1000–1700, Sun 1400–1700. Extended during the Festival in August
Admission	Free
Phone	031 556 8921

The gallery, one of Europe's most distinguished of its size, is housed in an imposing neo-classical building by William Playfair. The collection includes old Masters, Impressionist and Scottish paintings – works by Titian, Raphael, Rembrandt, Turner, Constable, El Greco, Van Gogh, Gauguin; and the Scottish masters, Ramsay, Raeburn and Wilkie.

The gallery also possesses around 19,000 prints, watercolours and drawings. Every January the Vaughan Bequest paintings by J. M. Turner are put on show.

The gallery hosts a series of temporary exhibitions and occasional concerts. School parties are welcomed. Facilities include a shop and a sales area; there is wheelchair access throughout.

Property	**PEOPLE'S PALACE**
Location	Glasgow Green, Glasgow, Strathclyde
Status	Local authority
Open	1000–1700, Sun 1400–1700
Admission	Free
Phone	041 554 0223

A first visit to this remarkable museum of social history is a revelation. The palace is devoted to the city's history and development from the foundations in the 1170s to the modern days of Billy Connolly.

The museum was opened in Glasgow's oldest public park in 1898 as a cultural centre for the people of the East End, and much of the material relates to 19th-century Glasgow.

There are displays on Mary, Queen of Scots and the Battle of Langside, the 18th-century tobacco lords and the history of the music hall. The museum has an absorbing collection of theatre posters and programmes, an array of trade union banners and artefacts concerned with the suffrage movement and the history of socialism in the city.

From the recent past there is a 1959 jukebox, a costume worn by Billy Connolly and displays on Glasgow's footballing tradition.

The history of the cinema is dealt with, and a collection of stained glass dating from 1850 to 1940 is particularly attractive.

The adjoining Winter Gardens, a large glasshouse, contains a wholefoods snack bar. There is a shop and partial access for wheelchairs.

Property	**THE PEOPLE'S STORY**
Location	Canongate Tolbooth, Edinburgh, Lothian
Status	Local authority
Open	1000–1700, summer closes 1800. Extended during the Festival in August
Admission	Free
Phone	031 225 2424

The People's Story is housed in one of the most picturesque buildings in the Royal Mile – a former courthouse and prison opposite Huntly House and built in 1591.

The museum exhibits material which reflects the social history of the Scottish capital from the late-18th century to the present day. It is filled with the sounds, sights and smells of everyday life. There is a prison cell, a model town crier, a re-enactment of a reform parade, a draper's shop, a fish wife, bookbinders' and coppers' workshops, a servant at work, a tramcar 'clippie', a 1940s kitchen, a 'steamie', a pub and a tea-room. There is an outstanding collection of trades union and polticial banners.

Facilities include a sales area and partial wheelchair access.

Property	# ROYAL MUSEUM OF SCOTLAND
Location	Chambers Street and Queen Street, Edinburgh, Lothian
Status	National Museums of Scotland
Open	1000–1700, Sun 1400–1700
Admission	Free
Phone	031 225 7534

The museum in Chambers Street houses the most comprehensive display under one roof in Britain. The main hall is a fine example of Victorian architecture, opened by Prince Albert in 1861. It contains Asiatic sculpture and the surrounding galleries exhibit ceramics, glass and silver. On the top floor is an excellent display of Chinese and Islamic decorative art.

There are international natural history rooms and a significant collection of minerals and fossils in the geology galleries.

There is an important Egyptian collection and the technology section includes 'Wylam Dilly', one of the oldest locomotives in existence.

The Queen Street building houses a staggering collection of Scottish material ranging from artefacts from Skara Brae to the Penicuik Jewels of Mary, Queen of Scots.

Both buildings offer full access to disabled visitors, sales areas and an active programme for schools. Chambers Street has a tea-room.

Property	# SCOTTISH NATIONAL GALLERY OF MODERN ART
Location	Belford Road, Edinburgh, Lothian
Status	National Galleries of Scotland
Open	1000–1700, Sun 1400–1700. Extended during the Festival in August
Admission	Free
Phone	031 556 8921

This gallery – housed in the former John Watson's School, a neo-classical building designed by William Burn in 1825 – is the most comprehensive of its type in Britain, apart from London's Tate Gallery. It contains Scotland's national collection of 20th-century paintings, sculpture and graphic art.

The collection, established in 1960, includes work by Picasso, Henry Moore, David Hockney, Braque, Hepworth, Lichtenstein, Matisse and Giacometti. Cadell, Redpath, Fergusson and Eardley are among the Scottish artists represented.

The gallery's library and print-room are accessible by appointment. Sculptures such as Moore's *Reclining Figure* are located in the grounds of the gallery.

Facilities include an educational service, coffee shop, sales area and temporary exhibitions, as well as full access for wheelchairs.

Property	# SCOTTISH NATIONAL PORTRAIT GALLERY
Location	Queen Street, Edinburgh, Lothian
Status	National Galleries of Scotland
Open	1000–1700, Sun 1400–1700
Admission	Free
Phone	031 556 8921

This impressive sandstone building relates the history of Scotland through portraits of famous men and women from the 16th century to the present day. They include Mary, Queen of Scots, Robert Burns, Sir Walter Scott, James VI, Ramsay MacDonald, David Hume and Flora MacDonald.

Many additional 'big names' from all walks of life are featured, and there is an outstanding collection of portraits by Ramsay, Reynolds, Raeburn and Gainsborough.

The exhibition also includes the Scottish photographic archive, including 5000 calotypes by Hill and Adamson, the photographic pioneers.

There is also a collection illustrating the development of Highland costumes. Facilities include a shop, temporary exhibitions and full wheelchair access.

FAMOUS SCOTS

Scotland has invented so many things and discovered so many places that the country's achievements have been printed for posterity on tea towels. Scots invented the telephone and the television, penicillin and the steamboat, and we have produced several great explorers, chief among them David Livingstone of Blantyre. A Scotsman founded the world's first savings bank, and another was the first governor of the Bank of England.

The scope of a second book would be needed to do merit to famous Scots. Here I have concentrated on the best known handful among the many whose portraits hang in the National Portrait Gallery. Burns, Scott and Buchan are household names. So are Bruce and Wallace. Once again whole holidays could revolve around visiting shrines to famous Scottish figures of the past.

Property	**ABBOTSFORD**
Location	A7, 2 m SSE of Galashiels, Borders
Status	Mrs P. Maxwell-Scott, OBE
Open	Mar–Oct, 1000–1700, Sun 1400–1700
Admission	Nominal charge, reduced rate for children
Phone	0896 2043

The romantic mansion house of the great Sir Walter Scott, Scotland's best-known novelist, is an important example of Scots Baronial architecture. It replaced Cartley Hole farmhouse on the right bank of the river Tweed, which Scott had bought in 1812.

Here the lawyer and author of the Waverley Novels entertained Wordsworth, Washington Irving and Thomas Moore. Scott was an enthusiastic collector of relics, and modern-day visitors to this important tourist venue can view such items as a model of the skull of Robert the Bruce, a clock belonging to Marie Antoinette, a clasp worn by Napoleon, some of Rob Roy's belongings, Montrose's sword, Prince Charles Edward Stuart's quaich and over 9000 rare books.

Abbotsford is inhabited by Scott's great, great, great grand-daughters, Dame Jean and Mrs Patricia Maxwell-Scott. The novelist himself died here in 1832, having written himself into the grave in an attempt to pay off his debts.

Facilities here include a tea-room and a shop. Access for wheelchairs is difficult.

Property	## JOHN BUCHAN CENTRE
Location	S end of Broughton, 5 m E of Biggar, Borders
Status	Biggar Museum Trust
Open	Easter–Oct, 1400–1700
Admission	Nominal charge, reduced rate for children
Phone	0899 21050

Set in charming Borders countryside on the tourist route from Moffat to Edinburgh, the John Buchan centre tells the life story of Buchan, the famous author of the crime thriller, *The Thirty-Nine Steps*.

Buchan's links with the village in Tweeddale began when his grandfather became tenant of a local farmhouse in 1851. Buchan's mother was born here, and he himself spent his summers as a child on holiday here. He became Lord Tweedsmuir, having distinguished himself in many fields. He was a lawyer, a politician, a soldier, a historian, a biographer and Governor-General of Canada.

Facilities include sales area and full access for wheelchairs.

Property	**BURNS COTTAGE AND MUSEUM**
Location	Alloway, 2 m S of Ayr, Strathclyde
Status	Trustees of Burns Monument
Open	Jun–Aug, 0900–1900, Apr, May, Sep, Oct, 1000–1700 (Sun 1400–1700) Nov–Mar, 1000–1600 (no Sun)
Admission	Nominal charge, reduced rate for children
Phone	0292 41215

Robert Burns, our national poet, was born in this thatched cottage on 25 January 1759, and he lived here until he was seven. The adjoining museum contains many Burnsian relics, books and manuscripts, and stands at the beginning of the Burns Heritage Trail. There is a large reference library.

Facilities include a tea-room, gift shop, museum and gardens, and information is available on cassette. Full wheelchair access.

Nearby are the Burns Monument and gardens. The Grecian monument was erected in 1823, and its museum has many relics associated with the bard. Nearby is the River Doon; there is also a gift-shop.

The Land o' Burns centre, an interpretation centre, stands on Murdoch's Lone, Alloway.

Property	**CARLYLE'S BIRTHPLACE**
Location	Ecclefechan, Dumfries and Galloway
Status	NTS
Open	Easter–Oct, 1200–1700
Admission	Nominal charge, reduced rate for children
Phone	057 63 666

Thomas Carlyle was born in 'the Arched House' on
4 December 1795, to become one of the most influential
thinkers of his generation. The house, built by
Carlyle's father and uncle who were masons, has been
carefully restored as a modest shrine to the man who
was known reverently as 'the Sage of Chelsea'. It was
handed over in 1936 by the Trustees of Carlyle's House
Memorial Fund, and completely refurbished in 1986.

Carlyle asked to be buried in the local cemetery,
rather than in Westminster Abbey along with the élite.

Exhibits at Carlyle's Birthplace include a collection
of Carlyle's belongings and manuscripts, and his
parents' clock still ticks away in the kitchen.
Wheelchair access is possible with assistance.

Property	**ELLISLAND FARM**
Location	A76 6 m NNW of Dumfries, Dumfries and Galloway
Status	Ellisland Trust
Open	All reasonable times
Admission	Free
Phone	0387 74 426

This farm, where our national bard, Robert Burns, lived from 1788 until 1791, stands on the right bank of the River Nith in Dunscore parish. Burns built the farmhouse in 1785, and it was here that he composed some of his masterpieces, including *Tam o' Shanter, Auld Lang Syne* and *John Anderson my Jo*, as he strolled along the river bank.

The farmhouse parlour is now a museum of the bard's relics, including his seal; letters; books; an initialled travelling case made out of a tree trunk; a shaving mirror and a fishing rod.

The granary was refurbished in 1979 as a museum of farming life, and contains a life-size model of the poet sowing oats from a sheet over his arm. There is a plough in the corner.

There is stepped access to the farmhouse.

Many tourists visit Dumfries to trace the life of Burns. Burns's House in Burns Street, the Burns Mausoleum in St Michael's churchyard, the Globe Inn in the High Street and the Robert Burns Centre on the right bank of the Nith are interesting ports of call.

Property	**JOHN KNOX HOUSE**
Location	High Street, Royal Mile, Edinburgh, Lothian
Status	Church of Scotland
Open	Mon–Sat 1000–1630
Admission	Nominal charge, reduced rate for children
Phone	031 556 6961

Number 45 High Street is an attractive-looking house, and is reputed to be the only 15th-century house in Scotland. The Scottish church reformer, John Knox, is associated with the house, and is said to have died here in 1572.

Knox, a former Roman Catholic priest, was a leading Protestant, and one of the founding figures of the Church of Scotland. A ten-minute video in the house tells the story of his life in Scotland and Switzerland. There is also an exhibition on his life and times

Renovation work revealed the original walls, fireplace and painted ceiling and the original floor in the Oak Room.

The house is also associated with James Mossman, the goldsmith who was keeper of the Royal Mint during the reign of Mary, Queen of Scots.

The house offers a puzzle trail for children and a sales area, as well as partial access for wheelchairs.

Property	**DAVID LIVINGSTONE CENTRE**
Location	Blantyre, Renfrewshire, Strathclyde
Status	Privately owned
Open	1000–1800, Sun 1400–1800
Admission	Nominal charge, reduced rate for children
Phone	0698 823140

Scotland's most famous explorer and missionary, David Livingstone, was born in 1813 in a single-room house in Shuttle Row, an 18th-century block of mill tenements. The block – on a bank of the River Clyde – is now the national memorial to Livingstone, and houses a collection of interesting relics of his life and work in Africa.

There is a permanent exhibition of maps and journals, and the adjacent social history museum deals with agriculture, mining and cotton spinning in the local area.

The Africa Pavilion hosts temporary exhibitions on modern Africa from April until September. There are eight acres of wooded parkland, a tea-room, a picnic area, gardens, play equipment and a paddling-pool. The centre offers partial access to disabled people.

Property	**SCOTT MONUMENT**
Location	Princes Street Gardens, Edinburgh, Lothian
Status	Local authority
Open	Apr–Sep, Mon–Fri 0900–1800 Oct–Mar, Mon–Fri 0900–1500
Admission	Nominal charge
Phone	031 225 2424

Built in memory of Scotland's greatest novelist in 1844, the Scott Monument is a landmark in the centre of the Scottish capital. It was based on the details and proportions of Melrose Abbey and designed by George Meikle Kemp.

The fantastic 200-feet high canopy and Gothic spire are decorated with statuettes of 64 characters from his novels. Underneath the canopy there is a statue of Scott and his dog, Maida, by Steele.

The top of the monument, reached by 287 steps, commands fine views of the city. It was closed for two years in March 1990 for renovation.

Scott was born in 1771 in a house near what is now Guthrie Street. He attended Edinburgh Royal High School and studied law at Edinburgh University.

Property	**WALLACE MONUMENT**
Location	A997, 1 m NNE of Stirling, Central
Status	Local authority
Open	Feb–Mar, Oct, 1000–1630, closed Wed, Thu Apr–Sep, 1000–1730, May–Aug, 1000–1830
Admission	Nominal charge, reduced rates for children & senior citizens
Phone	0786 72140

This 220-foot tower, a Scots totem pole, was designed by J. T. Rochead in memory of the patriot Sir William Wallace, who defeated the English at Stirling Bridge in 1297.

It was built between 1861 and 1869, and there is a statue of the famous Scot on the side of the tower. Inside the monument, Wallace's double-handed sword is preserved.

From the tower, seven battlefields can be seen, and there are superb views of Highland scenery. Inside there is a Hall of Heroes display and an exhibition on the life of Wallace, who was betrayed and suffered an agonising death at the hands of the English. There is also a 'sound and light' show on famous Scots.

Facilities include a cafe and woodland walks, but there is no access for wheelchairs.

SCOTLAND IN BLOOM

Gardens contribute so much to the enjoyment of a summer holiday that such creditable organisation as the National Trust for Scotland take them very seriously. As well as operating 23 attractive Scottish gardens, the Trust backs 'Scotland's Gardens Scheme', an independent charity founded in 1981. Under the scheme owners of wonderful gardens up and down the country open their properties on certain days and donate a percentage of the proceeds to charity.

The undernoted gardens, I hope, do justice to the magnificent variety in Scotland. Properties mentioned range from the mesmerising Inverewe Gardens in north-west Scotland to the formal and intricate Pitmedden – from neat little Priorwood to Threave, famed for its daffodils. All in all, Scotland is an oasis of floral beauty.

Property	**DUTHIE PARK WINTER GARDENS**
Location	Polmuir Road, Aberdeen, Grampian
Status	Local authority
Open	1000–dusk
Admission	Free
Phone	0224 583155

These exotic gardens, which were opened by Queen Victoria's youngest daughter, Princess Beatrice, in 1883, cover 44 acres of the 'Granite City', and contain several ponds, fountains, bowling greens and tennis courts. There is a reindeer park, a Japanese water garden, a cactus house, and centre for birds, fish and turtles.

In the centre of the park, there is an attractive Victorian bandstand, which is one of the best of its kind. The park also has a number of fascinating monuments, including one in memory of William Wallace, the patriot. There are sundials, Grecian sculptures and gargoyles. The plants come from Brazil, the Sandwich Islands, Natal, Mexico, Guyana, New Guinea and several other exotic countries.

Next to the restaurant there is a herd of wooden camels and a Celtic cross commemorating local victims of the Egyptian campaign of 1882.

Facilities include a tea-room, and the gardens have good access for wheelchairs and toilets for disabled people.

Property	**FINLAYSTONE ESTATE**
Location	A8, W of Langbank, Strathclyde
Status	Lady MacMillan
Open	0900–1700, Sun 1400–1700
Admission	Nominal charge, reduced rate for children
Phone	047 554 505/285

When Finlaystone was the seat of the Cunninghams, Earls of Glencairn, at different periods both John Knox and Robert Burns were visitors. Now the 80-acre estate is in the hands of the clan MacMillan, who had established beautiful gardens. One of the main attractions is the Celtic paving, a layout adapted from *The Book of Kells*, which comprises a series of floral circles and semi-circles.

The superb gardens bloom all the year round, and have done so since Lady MacMillan set them out in the 1930s. Particularly noteworthy are the herbaceous borders and the view of the River Clyde framed by plants. There are many fine trees, including examples of *Abies delavayi*.

Attractions in the mansion house include an amazing collection of dolls from throughout the world, and a Victorian exhibition of flower books.

Facilities on the estate include woodland walks with a ranger service, nursery gardens, adventure playground and picnic area. There is partial wheelchair access, a lift and toilets for disabled people. Afternoon teas are also available.

Property	**GLASGOW BOTANIC GARDENS**
Location	Great Western Road, Glasgow, Strathclyde
Status	Local authority
Open	Gardens 0700–dusk Kibble Palace, 1000–1645 summer (1615 winter)
Admission	Free
Phone	041 334 2422

These gardens, an institution in the city, were established in 1817 in a former university physick garden, but they were relocated on the present site 25 years later. The most outstanding feature is the Kibble Palace, a Victorian glasshouse with a famous collection of tree ferns. It is 23,000 square feet in area and is complemented by a number of Victorian sculptures.

Other glasshouses in the gardens boast a vast number of tropical plants, an internationally renowned collection of orchids and the 'National Collection' of begonias.

Forty acres of gardens are split into a Systematic Garden, a Herb Garden and a Chronological Border. There are footbridges across the River Kibble on the gardens' northern fringe.

There is wheelchair access to garden and grounds, and toilets for disabled people.

Property	**INVEREWE GARDENS**
Location	A832, Poolewe, Ross and Cromarty
Status	NTS
Open	Gardens: 0930–sunset Centre and shop: 1 Apr–4 May, Mon–Sat 1000–1700; 5 Sep–23 Oct, Mon–Sat 1000–1700, Sun 1200–1700; 5 May–4 Sep, Mon–Sat 1000–1830, Sun 1200–1700
Admission	Nominal charge, reduced rate for children
Phone	044 586 200

These gardens, stretching over 50 acres, are like an oasis amid the rugged countryside of the Western Highlands. They are set on a peninsula on the shores of Loch Ewe. They were established by Osgood Mackenzie in 1864 when he planted pines and rhododendron hedges to shelter his project.

The beneficial Gulf Stream allows the gardens to grow rare and sub-tropical plants on a latitude north of Moscow. Notable features include the rhododendrons, eucalyptuses and many south American plants. There are Himalayan lilies, and giant forget-me-nots from the south Pacific.

Inverewe Gardens boast a good range of visitor services including a visitor centre, a caravan and camping site, a garden for disabled people, and a restaurant.

The ranger service operates during July and August.

Property	**LOGAN BOTANIC GARDEN**
Location	B7065, 14 m S of Stranraer, Dumfries and Galloway
Status	State-owned
Open	Mar–Oct 1000–1800
Admission	Nominal charge, reduced rate for children & senior citizens
Phone	077 686 231

Logan Botanic Garden, an outstation of the Royal Botanic Garden in Edinburgh, is the most southerly in Scotland. It boasts many rare plants from the southern hemisphere, and – unusually for Scotland – the Gulf Stream and the mild climate of the Rhinns of Galloway allow it to grow exotic plants without glasshouses.

Oddities include cabbage palms, tree ferns, Californian lilies, Japanese irises, which grow a mile or so from the stormy Irish Sea and the same distance from placid Luce Bay.

To the west of the showpiece-tree ferns stand the ruins of the old castle of Balzieland. The woodland area features the largest outdoor Brazilian Gunnera manicata in Britain. Elsewhere there are passion-flowers, lobelias, hydrangeas and poplars.

The McDoualls of Logan, one of Scotland's oldest families, lived here from the 12th century until 1945, when the estate went to Sir Ninian Buchan-Hepburn.

Facilities include a licensed salad bar, access for disabled people, and a car park.

Property	**PITMEDDEN GARDEN**
Location	B999 14 m NW of Aberdeen, Grampian
Status	NTS
Open	0930 to sunset Museum open summer
Admission	Nominal charge, reduced rate for children, additional charge for museum
Phone	065 13 2352

This is a magnificent formal geometric garden within a walled square and divided into four. One of the quarters has a floral saltire and thistle, and the coat-of-arms of the Setons, lairds of Pitmedden. Another has a sundial and floral depiction of the well-known Latin dictum, *tempus fugit* (time flies).

The garden, with its pavilions and fountains and manicured look, was established by Sir Alexander Seton in 1675 and lovingly restored by the Trust. One of the notable features is the eastern half of the square modelled on the Charles II garden at the Palace of Holyroodhouse in Edinburgh.

Pitmedden House also has a museum of family life with a collection of farming tools and domestic utensils. There are also woodland walks on the 100-acre estate, as well as an exhibition on formal gardens. Facilities include a ranger service, a picnic area, a tea-room, a visitor centre and partial access for wheelchair users and a toilet for disabled people, a wheelchair is also available.

Property	**PRIORWOOD GARDEN**
Location	A6091 nr Melrose Abbey, Borders
Status	NTS
Open	Apr–Oct 1000–1730 Winter 1000–1730, closed Sun
Admission	By donation
Phone	089 682 2965

Priorwood Garden, within sight of Melrose Abbey, one of Scotland's most splendid ruins, is a tempting place in which to linger – among delphiniums and over 700 other floral wonders. All the plants in the beautiful walled garden are grown to be dried by a group of Trust volunteers. Visitors may watch them hard at work. Drying techniques used *in situ* range from the ancient Egyptian method of sand-drying to the modern use of a microwave oven.

In a small orchard within the garden there is an 'Apples Through the Ages' theme. Adjacent stands a tourist information centre run jointly with the Scottish Borders Tourist Board.

Facilities include picnic tables and a shop. Wheel-chair access is possible with assistance.

Property	## ROYAL BOTANIC GARDENS, EDINBURGH
Location	Inverleith Row, Edinburgh, Lothian
Status	State-owned
Open	*Summer*, grounds Mon–Sat 0900–one hour before sunset, Sun 1100 to one hour before sunset Planthouses: Mon–Sat 1000–1700, Sun 1100–1700 *Winter*, grounds 0900 to dusk Planthouses: Mon–Sat 1000 to dusk Sun 1100 to dusk Extended opening during the Festival in August
Admission	Free
Phone	031 552 7171

These well-known gardens specialise in the conservation of threatened plants from throughout the world, and they are thought to possess the largest collection of rhododendrons in the world.

There is a world-famous rock garden containing unique alpine plants and a range of exotic species.

At the end of the 18th century, plants poured in from the colonies, especially from southern Africa. Today heath gardens contain numerous rare heath plants.

An exhibition hall houses botanical and horticultural displays. Other facilities include a tea-room, a shop and facilities for disabled people.

Property	**THREAVE GARDENS**
Location	A75, 1 m of Castle Douglas, Dumfries and Galloway
Status	NTS
Open	0900–sunset, walled garden/ glasshouse 0900–1700
Admission	Nominal charge, reduced rate for children
Phone	0556 2575

The Trust founded a horticultural school in Threave, a Victorian mansion-house, in 1960, and the 60-acre garden is now recognised internationally for its layout and collection. They grow 200 varieties of daffodils at Threave in the spring, and the old walled garden contains a selection of fruit and vegetables.

The peat and woodland gardens are ablaze with colour in springtime, while the rock garden blooms from May until June. The rose garden and herbaceous beds attract visitors in the late summer and the heath garden shows a good colour in the autumn.

A formal garden opened in 1990, and in it six different period gardens have been created. The adjacent wildfowl refuge is a roosting place for many species of wildfowl during the winter. It sits on the river Dee. There is access from November to March with guided tours by a ranger.

Facilities at Threave include a tea-room, shop and toilets for disabled people. There is partial wheelchair access.

Property	**YOUNGER BOTANIC GARDEN**
Location	A815, 7 m NNW of Dunoon, Strathclyde
Status	State-owned
Open	Apr–Oct 1000–1800
Admission	Nominal charge, reduced rate for children & senior citizens
Phone	0369 6261

These attractive gardens are an out-station of the Royal Botanic Garden in Edinburgh. They contain more than 250 different species of azaleas and rhododendrons, many from the Himalayas and the Far East. There are 'lantern trees' and Sierra redwoods in the extensive woodlands.

The redwood avenue, which visitors will see when they enter the gates, were planted by Piers Patrick, who owned the then estate of Benmore from 1862 until 1870. A later owner, James Duncan, planted six million trees on the estate.

The gardens were owned by a member of the Younger brewing family until the 1920s, when they were gifted to the nation. Nowadays botanists at the garden undertake research into rhododendrons, berberis and conifers, while visitors stroll along a good network of footpaths. There is a tea-room, a car park and toilets for disabled people.

Royal Botanic Gardens, Edinburgh.

SCOTLAND:
THE GREAT OUTDOORS

Scotland possesses some of the world's finest walking
and climbing terrain; indeed, if we had the weather of
the Mediterranean, we would 'clean up' in terms of
tourism.

One of the benefits of rambling in Scotland is the
moral freedom to roam the hills, a concept absent in
England. Scotland *does* have a law of trespass, but
there is a *de facto* right to walk unimpeded which, if
removed, would result in an unprecedented public
outcry.

Ramblers and hillwalkers, however, have a duty to
observe the country code – to shut gates properly, to
keep dogs on a leash if there are sheep around, and to
stay away from shooting areas during the season.
Dropping litter, especially glass, is a senseless thing to
do.

Scotland has some of Europe's most precious
wildlife havens and walkers should be sensitive to the
needs of flora and fauna. In particular, St Kilda is of
global ecological importance, and the Nature
Conservancy Council (NCC) operates some 40
National Nature Reserves where wildlife is conserved.

The Roman poet Horace wrote that you could drive
Nature out with a pitchfork, but it would keep coming
back. The NCC, wary of this thinking, shield animals
and such majestic birds as the golden eagle and the
osprey from the 'pitchforks' of human encroachment.

Property	**ADEN COUNTRY PARK**
Location	A950 between Mintlaw and New Deer, Grampian
Grid Ref	NJ982478
Status	Local authority
Admission	Free
Phone	0771 22857

Aden Country Park boasts 230 acres of beautiful woodland and farmland, the grounds of an old estate. There are nature trails and a network of footpaths with wheelchair access to the gardens.

The grounds are the setting for the award-winning North-East Scotland Agricultural Heritage where two centuries of farming heritage are brought to life. The Aden Estate Story, an exhibition, depicts life in the community in the 1920s, and there are regular exhibitions of vintage farm machinery, Clydesdale horses and so on.

A new Wildlife Discovery Centre opened in May 1990 within a former coach-house and stables. Schoolchildren can view an audio-visual display entitled Woodland Walks and Puddocks.

Facilities include a ranger service, a picnic area, a restaurant, a shop and an adventure playground.

Property	**BEINN EIGHE** National Nature Reserve
Location	W of A896/A832 junction Kinlochewe, Highland
Grid Ref	NG000610
Status	Nature Conservancy Council (NCC)
Admission	Free
Phone	044 584 258/244

Beinn Eighe was declared Britain's first National Nature Reserve in 1951 and is of great geological, scenic and natural history interest. The reserve covers over 10,000 acres of spectacular moorland and mountains, natural pine and birchwoods. The pines along Loch Maree (*Glas Leitire* – the wood on the grey slope) is a remnant of the Caledonian Forest.

There are many birds to be seen, including eagles, peregrines, ptarmigan, black grouse, crossbills and red and black-throated divers.

There is a visitor centre at Aultroy Cottage on the A832; a car park, toilets and nature trails, as well as partial wheelchair access. Access to the reserve is restricted during autumn.

Property	**BEN LAWERS** National Nature Reserve
Location	6 m NE of Killin, Tayside
Grid Ref	NN6341
Status	NTS
Admission	Visitor centre: Nominal charge, reduced rate for children Open Apr–Sep, 1000–1700
Phone	056 72 397

A climber's dream, Ben Lawers is Perthshire's highest mountain, and it affords panoramic views from the North Sea to the Atlantic Ocean. In 1950 the Trust bought nearly 8000 acres of the southern slopes, which is a prime site for rare birds and plants. They are the domain of buzzards, kestrels, red grouse, curlews and cuckoos. The ledges, scree and corries of this lime-rich doyen of the Breadalbane range support a number of rare plants, including snow gentian and alpine forget-me-nots.

Ranger services are available.

Property	**BEN LOMOND**
Location	Rowardennan, Central
Grid Ref	NN367029
Status	NTS
Admission	Free
Phone	No

Ben Lomond is one of Scotland's best-known, and most popular, mountains. It rises to 3194 ft from the eastern shore of Loch Lomond (Britain's largest area of freshwater). Not suprisingly it offers the climber picture-postcard panoramas of Ayrshire, Arran and Ailsa Craig, the Arrochar alps, Ben Nevis and Loch Katrine.

The summits of Sron Aonaich (1893 ft), Beinn Uird (1955 ft) and Ptarmigan (2398 ft) are all within 5423 acres bought by the Trust in 1984.

Ramblers are warned to keep any dogs on leads, for this is sheep-farming country. There are no ranger services; nor is there a visitor centre – simply hills to climb, roam and contemplate.

Property	**CAERLAVEROCK** National Nature Reserve
Location	B725 S of Dumfries, Dumfries and Galloway
Grid Ref	NY051656
Status	NCC
Admission	Free Wildfowl refuge: Nominal charge, reduced rate for children & senior citizens
Phone	038 777 275

This salt marsh on the Solway coast is one of Britain's most important wintering grounds for wildfowl and plays host each year to the entire world population of Spitzbergen barnacle geese. The reserve stretches over 14,000 acres of land once owned by the Duke of Norfolk, and was the location of Scotland's first national wildfowl refuge – and the first in Britain to allow conservation and shooting to run hand-in-hand.

A refuge and visitor centre is run by the Wildfowl and Wetlands Trust on 100 acres of the reserve, at Eastpark Farm. The refuge boasts some of the best facilities in the country for viewing birds close at hand. There are excellent observation towers and hide facilities. Children can see swans coming in to land gracefully on the pool.

There is wheelchair access on the ground floor.

Property	**EDINBURGH BUTTERFLY AND INSECT WORLD**
Location	Melville Nurseries, Lasswade, Lothian
Grid Ref	- NT3065
Status	Dobbies' Garden Centre
Admission	Nominal charge, reduced rates for children & senior citizens
Phone	031 663 4932

Whatever the weather, visitors will enjoy strolling through Scotland's largest garden centre. There is a reconstruction of a tropical rainforest landscaped with exotic plants, cascading waterfalls and lily-ponds. Butterflies from many countries flutter around in this artificial habitat. They are spectacular and very colourful.

At close quarters, but in safety, visitors can observe praying mantis and stick insects. The place is, understandably, a hit with the children.

There is an adventure playground, as well as a tropical fish shop and a picnic area.

Property	**GOAT FELL**
Location	Isle of Arran, Strathclyde
Grid Ref	NR992416
Status	NTS
Admission	Free
Phone	No

The skyline which travellers on the Arran ferry are privileged to witness on a clear evening probably represents the most awe-inspiring approach to any Scottish island.

The vista – minus the sea – would not be out of place in Switzerland, even Afghanistan. Goat Fell, the highest mountain, is flanked by the jagged peaks of Ben Nuis, Cir Mhor, Ben Tarsuinn and the Sleeping Warrior.

Although Goat Fell is not a Munro (a mountain over 3000 feet in height), it sprouts from sea level and is a fair climb. A visitor could spend a week of happy exploring the range, which provides some marvellously daunting ascents and great ridge walks.

Goat Fell is something of an institution, perhaps because of its dominance of the skyline over Brodick, perhaps because of its accessibility.

The Trust owns 6603 acres, including part of Glen Rosa and Cir Mhor (2618 feet, but difficult to negotiate).

There is a visitor centre at the adjacent Brodick Castle, and a good ranger service.

Property	**GREY MARE'S TAIL**
Location	10 m NE of Moffat, Dumfries and Galloway
Grid Ref	NT191149
Status	NTS
Admission	Free
Phone	No

The Grey Mare's Tail is a spectacular waterfall, and one of the main attractions in Dumfriesshire's most rugged tract of countryside, the Moffat hills. The surrounding hills are dramatic moorland, which were once a place of refuge for fugitive Covenanters, and the stamping-ground of Sir Walter Scott and James Hogg, 'the Ettrick Shepherd'.

The 'tail' cascades over 200 feet from a superb example of a hanging valley at Loch Skeen, at 1700 feet one of Scotland's highest lochs. This is an area beloved by hill-walkers, but many people just park their cars in the park at the foot of the hill and take the pleasant walk up to the waterfall. The area also has rare plants and is a mecca for geologists and ornithologists.

The Trust owns over 2500 acres, including Dobb's Linn, which was purchased in 1972.

There are information boards about the geological effects of glaciation and so on in the car park. Feral goats can be seen on the hills, but the Trust advises walkers to keep to the path, since there have been several deaths here.

A ranger service operates during July and August.

Property	**KINTAIL AND MORVICH**
Location	16 m E of Kyle of Lochalsh, Highland
Grid Ref	NG961211
Status	NTS
Admission	By donation Visitor centre (unattended) open: 25 May–30 Sep, Mon–Sat 1000–1800, Sun 1400–1800
Phone	059 981 219

This is a magnificent swathe of beautiful Highland countryside, dominated by the spectacular Beinn Fhada and the equally impressive Five Sisters of Kintail, all but one a gnarled Munro rising to around 3500 feet. The 'Sisters' form the western side of a 20-mile ridge running from Loch Duich to Glen Moriston.

The ridge attracts many climbers and the corries are home to herds of red deer and feral goats.

The Trust owns 15,000 acres including a countryside centre at Morvich farm, off the A87. Access to the mountains is best from this point. The site of the battle Glen Shiel, which was fought in 1719, is situated five miles east of the village beside the main road.

There is a Trust caravan site at Morvich, which is open between 3 March and 8 October. Fishing is available and, there is a ranger service.

Property	**LOCH GARTEN**
Location	off B970 E of Boat of Garten, Highland
Grid Ref	NH978184
Status	Royal Society for the Protection of Birds
Admission	Free; shop and hide open: Apr–Aug 1000–2000 Reserve open all year round
Phone	0479 83694

Loch Garten is famous as a breeding sanctuary for ospreys, which were re-introduced to Scotland in 1959 after becoming extinct. Visitors can view their tree-top eyrie through fixed binoculars at an observation-hut.

The reserve is blessed with one of only three surviving tracts of Caledonian pine forest, which provides a habitat for crested tits, Scottish crossbills, capercaillies, goldeneyes and other threatened species.

Ospreys can be spotted from the end of April until August, but the surrounding landscapes can be appreciated at any time of year, particularly in February and March. At this time visitors are often fortunate enough to observe the eccentric courting ritual of the male capercaillie, or see some of the rarer visitors such as waxwings and great grey shrikes.

Facilities on the reserve include a shop and a hide. Naturally access to the reserve is regulated during certain crucial periods.

Property	**JOHN MUIR COUNTRY PARK**
Location	W of Dunbar, Lothian
Grid Ref	NT640800
Status	Local authority
Admission	Free
Phone	0620 842637

Scotland's first country park of its kind – an eight-mile stretch of coastline – is named after John Muir, the native of Dunbar who emigrated to America and became a pioneering conservationist. He also founded the Yosemite and Sequoia Parks, which were the basis of the American National Park system.

John Muir Country Park includes a large area of attractive sandy beach and foreshore, and the estuary of the River Tyne. Most of the area, which takes in Belhaven Bay and Ravensheugh Sands, is designated a Site of Special Scientific Interest (SSSI). There is a good clifftop nature trail commanding views of the Isle of May and Bass Rock. The area has considerable conservation value, although it has a golf course and a caravan site.

There is a wide variety of habitats, attracting wild flowers, common-blue and meadow-brown butterflies, migrant whimbrels and greenshank.

There is a ranger service. Access points are off the north side of the A1087 at West Barns and off the east side of the A198 half a mile north of the village of Tyninghame.

Property	**ST ABB'S HEAD** National Nature Reserve
Location	off B6438 N of Coldingham, Borders
Grid Ref	NT914688
Status	Scottish Wildlife Trust/NTS
Admission	By donation
Phone	089 07 71443

This rugged and stimulating coastal headland near Eyemouth has cliffs rising to 300 feet and is an important migration observation point well-known for its breeding and migrating seabirds. It is the most important site for cliff-nesting seabirds in south-east Scotland.

Guillemots, kittiwakes, razorbills, shags, fulmars and herring gulls crowd the promontory of lava between May and October, while Manx shearwaters can be spotted in autumn. Puffins are often seen – as are purple sandpipers and turnstones.

Notable migrants are the red-backed shrike, the red-breasted flycatcher and the wryneck.

The reserve boasts many wild flowers – and grand views out to the North Sea.

Facilities include a ranger service, a car park and a tea-room. There are official viewpoints, and partial wheelchair access.

Property	**ST KILDA**
Location	110 m W of Scottish mainland
Grid Ref	NF0999
Status	NTS leases to NCC
Admission	Free
Phone	031 226 5922

A visit to this remarkable group of islands on the edge of Europe is the experience of a lifetime. The remote archipelago has the highest cliffs in Britain (1397 feet) and the world's largest gannetry (50,000 pairs).

The islands comprising the first place in Scotland to be designated by UNESCO A World Heritage Site are Berneray, Dun, Hirta, Soay (famous for its sheep), Stac Lee and Stac an Armin.

St Kilda was evacuated on Friday, 29 August 1930, her inhabitants having lived on seabirds and their eggs for centuries. The Nature Conservancy Council declared the islands a National Nature Reserve in 1957, and UNESCO accepted them as being of global importance in 1986.

Ornithologists travel to St Kilda in great numbers because it is one of Europe's most important breeding grounds for a number of species. There are thousands of gannets, fulmars, guillemots, razorbills, kittiwakes and puffins. The fulmar colony is Britain's oldest, and the 300,000 puffins represent by far the majority of the British total.

St Kilda has it own species of wren and mouse. There are 125 pairs of wrens, although there were only 15 in 1894.

Property	**TORRIDON**
Location	Ross and Cromarty, Highland
Grid Ref	NG9056
Status	NTS
Admission	Deer museum: Nominal charge, reduced rate for children Audio-visual display by donation Visitor centre (unattended) open: 25 May–30 Sep, Mon–Sat 1000–1800, Sun 1400–1800
Phone	044 587 221

This majestic geological masterpiece is one of
Scotland's great wildernesses, and the Trust owns
16,100 acres of the quartz and sandstone stacks, which
form the country's most frightening mountain scenery.

Torridonian sandstone is up to 750 million years old,
and Torridon used to lie south of the equator. It is now
a lot colder. Replete with several Munros, including
Liathach (3456 feet and with seven tops) and Beinn
Alligin (3232 feet), it is, nevertheless, one of the
spiritual homes of mountaineers and naturalists in
Scotland.

Facilities include a deer museum, open all year, and
an unmanned visitor centre which is open from 25 May
until 30 September, Mon–Sat 1000–1800, Sun 1400–1800.

A good ranger service is headed by Lea MacNally
BEM, one of the leading authorities on red deer and
golden eagles.

SCOTLAND AT WORK

Some of the best produce you will find came out of Scotland: much of it is amber and comes by the bottle. Whisky is Scotland's national drink, and the beverage has a fascinating history of its own. This section deals with ten distilleries, eight of which are on Speyside, the 'homeland' of the water of life.

Also included is New Lanark, that landmark of social history in the Clyde Valley – the best surviving example in the country of an industrial village.

Glen Grant Distillery

Property	**BAXTERS OF SPEYSIDE**
Location	0.5 m W of Fochabers, Grampian
Status	W A Baxter and Sons Ltd
Open	Mar–Dec, 1000–1700
Admission	Free
Phone	0343 820 393

Baxters have been carving a name for themselves in the manufacture of soups and other quality foods for over 100 years. The family-owned business is on the so-called 'Scotland's Quality Trail', and supplies customers in over 60 countries.

Visitors are given a guided tour of the factory and an audio-visual display entitled The Baxters' Story. There is a cellar, a Victorian kitchen and the old shop where the company first set up shop making their famous soups.

Facilities also include the Spey Restaurant and a display of Highland cattle. There is wheelchair access.

Property	**CROMBIE WOOLLEN MILL**
Location	A96 Woodside, Aberdeen, Grampian
Status	J and J Crombie Ltd
Open	0900–1630, Sun 1200–1630
Admission	Free
Phone	0224 483201

Situated in rural surroundings on the bank of the river Don three miles from Aberdeen, the Grandholm Mill is the home of the world-famous Crombie cloths. John Crombie founded the business nearly 200 years ago, and travelled to London on horseback to sell his wares.

Now Crombies claim to have the largest and best equipped woollen mill in Scotland, selling 'the world's finest cloths'.

The visitor centre depicts life at the mill since the 1800s, and the latest fashion trends can be viewed in the showroom.

Facilities include the Spinning Jenny Restaurant and Coffee Shop, a picnic area and riverside walks.

Property	**GLENTURRET DISTILLERY**
Location	The Hosh, Crieff, Tayside
Status	Glenturret Distillery Limited
Open	Mar–Dec, Mon–Sat 0930–1630 Jan–Feb, Mon–Fri, 1130–1430
Admission	Nominal charge, reduced rate for children, audio-visual display extra
Phone	0764 2424

Glenturret Distillery is arguably Scotland's oldest – dating back to 1775 – and is a popular tourist venue. The reception centre has won awards, and features a three-dimensional exhibition museum, tasting bar and restaurant. There is also a shop for souvenir-hunters.

The distillery uses pure water from the Turret Burn to manufacture award-winning malts – 8, 12, 15 and 21-year-olds. The distillery cat, Towser, was a celebrity until it died, aged 23, in March 1987. Towser held the world mouse-catching record. She had caught over 28,000 rodents before departing for the great distillery in the sky.

MALT WHISKY TRAIL, SPEYSIDE

To many Speyside is the traditional heartland of the malt whisky industry – simply because so many high-quality whiskies are manufactured there. Speyside is the so-called 'Golden Triangle' wherein lies the largest concentration of malt-whisky-making equipment in the world.

On Speyside you can travel along the world's only Malt Whisky Trail. Visitors follow a clearly signposted trail, which calls in at eight distilleries. Approximately one hour is advised at each distillery. Do not drink too many free drams, and take along that invaluable bible of malt whiskies, *Wallace Milroy's Malt Whisky Almanac* (Lochar Publishing).

Property	CARDHU
Location	B9102, Knockando
Status	United Distillers
Open	Mon–Fri 0930–1630, Sat (Easter–Oct)
Admission	Free
Phone	03406 204

At Cardhu you can hear how the founder's wife, Helen Cumming, used to hoist a red flag from the barn to warn crofters on the hills that the exciseman was on the lookout for their illicit stills.

Facilities include a coffee shop, themed display and souvenir shop.

Property	**GLENFARCLAS**
Location	A95, 17 m WSW of Keith
Status	J and G Grant
Open	Mon–Fri 0900–1630 (weekends Jun–Sep, Sat 1000–1600, Sun 1300–1600)
Admission	Free
Phone	08072 245/257

Well-known distillery with roots in a family tradition going back to 1835. The brochure quotes a professional taster as saying – of the whisky: 'It goes down singing hymns'.

Facilities include a gift shop, audio-visual display, whisky exhibition in four languages, cask-filling gallery and picnic area. There is wheelchair access with assistance.

Property	**GLENFIDDICH**
Location	A941 N of Dufftown
Status	Wm Grant and Sons Ltd.
Open	Mon–Fri 0930–1630, Easter–Oct, Sat 0930–1630, Sun 1200–1630
Admission	Free
Phone	0340 20373

This is the only distillery in the Highlands where malt whisky is bottled on the premises. It has an extremely popular reception centre, with wheelchair access. There is an audio-visual programme in six languages.

Property	**GLEN GRANT**
Location	Rothes
Status	The Seagram Co Ltd
Open	Mid Apr–Sep, Mon–Fri 1000–1600
Admission	Free
Phone	03403 413

Established in 1840 by James and John Grant, it was then the largest producer on Speyside. Facilities include a gift shop and an audio-visual display.

Property	**GLENLIVET**
Location	B9008 10 m N of Tomintoul
Status	The Seagram Co Ltd
Open	Easter–Oct, Mon–Sat 1000–1600
Admission	Free
Phone	08073 427

First licensed distillery in the Highlands (1824), following the 1823 Act of Parliament, which reduced illicit distilling and smuggling.

Facilities include a gift shop, audio-visual display, coffee shop, picnic area, and exhibition with partial access and a special toilet for disabled people.

Property	**STRATHISLA**
Location	Keith
Status	The Seagram Co Ltd
Open	Mid May–mid Sep, Mon–Fri 0900–1630
Admission	Free
Phone	05422 7471

A typical small old-fashioned distillery. One of the oldest in Scotland, it dates from 1786.

Facilities include audio-visual display, reception centre and partial wheelchair access, as well as a special toilet for disabled people.

Property	**TAMDHU**
Location	B9012 8 m W of Craigiellachie
Status	The Highland Distilleries Co Ltd
Open	Easter–end May, Mon–Fri 1000–1600, June–Sep Mon–Sat 1000–1600
Admission	Free
Phone	03406 486

A viewing gallery houses a unique collection of over 130 different whiskies. Facilities include a gift shop, picnic area and small exhibition. There are views of the distillery plant from the gallery.

Property	**TAMNAVULIN**
Location	Ballindalloch
Status	The Invergordon Distillers Ltd.
Open	Mar–Oct 0930–1630, Jun–Sep also Sun 1030–1630
Admission	Free
Phone	08073 442

The Old Mill Visitor Centre was built originally as a wool-carding mill. Situated in picturesque setting on the banks of the River Livet. Facilities include a gift shop and picnic area. There is partial wheelchair access as well as a special toilet for disabled people.

Property	# NEW LANARK VILLAGE
Location	0.5 m S of Lanark, Strathclyde
Status	Trustees
Open	All reasonable times Centre 1100–1700
Admission	Nominal charge, reduced rates for children
Phone	0555 61345

New Lanark, a 200-year-old cotton-spinning village, is the best example in Scotland of an industrial village. Nestling in the wooded Clyde Valley, it is a product of the Industrial Revolution – built by David Dale and Richard Arkwright. They erected four mills and houses for over 1500 workers between 1788 and 1799.

Dale's son-in-law, Robert Owen, became famous as a social reformer through his innovative management techniques. The village was the cradle of the co-operative movement. Education at the Institute for the Formation of Character replaced child labour.

The buildings are all grade-A listed. The old institute has been converted as a reception area, which holds educational exhibitions. Laser and hologram technology is used in the visitor centre, and there is working 19th-century spinning equipment.

Facilities also include a Scottish Wildlife Trust visitor centre, picnic and play areas. There is partial wheelchair access. New Lanark was nominated as a World Heritage Site.

Property	**ROYAL LOCHNAGAR**
Location	A93 at Crathie, Ballater, Grampian
Status	United Distillers
Open	Apr–Oct, Mon–Fri 0930–1700, Sat 1000–1700, Sun 1100–1600
Admission	Free
Phone	033 84 273

When John Begg cheekily invited his neighbours to come and get a dram at his new distillery in 1845, to his astonishment they accepted. They were none other than Queen Victoria and Prince Albert. The whole Royal Family, tradition has it, came down from Balmoral Castle to taste Begg's *uisge beatha*.

Three years later the Queen granted Begg a royal warrant: so pleased was she with his produce.

Visitors to Balmoral often call into the distillery to see how the 12-year-old single Highland malt is made. An added attraction is the model of an illicit still – tended by a dummy bootlegger.

The tour takes you through the mash house to the vast fermentation casks and into the impressive still-house. Then it's the free dram. *Slainte*!

ROYAL
LOCHNAGAR

SELECTED RESERVE

Single Highland Malt

SCOTCH WHISKY

Produced in Scotland

BY

Royal Lochnagar Distillery

CRATHIE, DEESIDE
ABERDEENSHIRE
SCOTLAND

75cl   43% Vol

ESTD   1845

The diary of John Begg   *14th September 1848*

'I asked Prince Albert if he would like to taste a dram.
H.R.H. having agreed to this, I called for a bottle and glasses
(which had been previously in readiness) and, presenting one
glass to Her Majesty, she tasted it. So did His Royal Highness
the Prince. I then presented a glass to the Princess Royal, and
to the Prince of Wales, and Prince Alfred, all of whom tasted
the spirit.'

As a result of this visit the Distillery was granted the
privilege of calling itself 'Royal' Lochnagar, the very first to
be accorded this honour by Her Majesty

MISCELLANEOUS SCOTLAND

The last section deals with special interest destinations. It might seem a little perverse to bracket the prehistoric settlements of Skara Brae and Jarlshof along with the Loch Ness Monster, but each of the following eight entries is sufficiently offbeat to deserve inclusion in a mixed bag.

Here we have eerie Inveraray Jail, where old lags come back to haunt you; The Famous Old Blacksmiths' Shop, where umpteen couples have taken their marriage vows, and the Scotch Whisky Heritage Centre, which takes you on a journey through the centuries. Anderson's Storybook Glen is a *must* for hard-to-please children. Happy holidays!

Property	**STORYBOOK GLEN**
Location	Maryculter, 5 m WSW of Aberdeen, Grampian
Status	Family run
Open	Mar–Oct, 1000–1800
Admission	Nominal charge, reduced rate for children
Phone	0224 732941

Storybook Glen is a child's delight – and the result of 11 years' work and is peopled by storybook characters such as Snow White and the Seven Dwarves, the Three Bears and The Old Woman who Lived in a Shoe.

The glen is on a 22-acre site landscaped by waterfalls and banks of rhododendrons and azaleas. Robinson Crusoe has his island there, and there is Little Miss Muffet and Little Boy Blue. The children adore Old MacDonald's Farm and Postman Pat.

Property	CLAN DONALD CENTRE
Location	Armadale, Isle of Skye, Highland
Status	Clan Donald Trust
Open	18 Mar–2 Nov, 0930–1730
Admission	Nominal charge, reduced rate for children & senior citizens
Phone	047 14 305

This award-winning visitor centre at the southern end of the Sleat peninsula (the Garden of Skye), is set in 40 acres of restored 19th-century gardens and woodlands. It is a focal point for clansmen from all over the world, especially the 'sons of Donald', thousands of whom stay in the United States and Canada.

The oldest part of Armadale Castle houses the Museum of the Isles exhibition, and an audio-visual programme relates the history of the Lords of the Isles and the story of the Gaelic kingdom. A new library and study centre house significant historical records and information on genealogy. The stables in which the Donald lords used to keep their steeds have been converted into a licensed restaurant and a gift shop. Visitors can explore the woodlands, moorland and coastline with a countryside ranger – minutes from the Armadale ferry-point. First-class accommodation is also available at the centre.

Facilities include a shop and a restaurant, and wheelchairs are available on loan.

Property	**FAMOUS OLD BLACKSMITH'S SHOP**
Location	Gretna Green, off A74, Dumfries and Galloway
Status	Gretna Museum and Tourist Services
Open	Jan–Feb, 1000–1600; Mar–May, 0900–1700; Jun–Sep, 0900–2000; Oct–Dec, 0900–1700
Admission	Nominal charge
Phone	0461 38441/38224

Gretna Green is now largely devoted to 'mock weddings' over the anvil, but the village used to be a mecca for runaway lovers, who wanted to take advantage of the more convenient marriage laws of Scotland.

The Famous Old Blacksmith's Shop became renowned as a wedding venue: couples would knock on the blacksmith's door – even during the night – to ask to be married. The 'shop' has entertained King George V, Queen Mary, King Hussein of Jordan, the Sultan of Muscat, Lloyd George and a host of film and showbusiness people. The modern-day visitor centre has a collection of old coaches, including one used by King William IV and Queen Adelaide (Queen Victoria's aunt). There is an enormous shop, selling everything from food to fabrics, a restaurant and a bar; easy wheelchair access, plus a toilet for disabled people.

Property	**INVERARAY JAIL**
Location	Inveraray, Argyll, Strathclyde
Status	Local authority-owned. Leased by Visitor Centres Ltd, Landmark
Open	0930–1800, Winter 1000–1700
Admission	Nominal charge, reduced rate for children & senior citizens
Phone	0499 2381

One of Scotland's most bizarre tourist attractions, Inveraray Jail is the first 19th-century prison and courthouse in Europe to be opened to the public. Visitors can go behind bars and see what it was like to be on the receiving end of justice. Life-like figures, furnished cells, imaginative exhibitions, sounds and smells all bring the jail back to life. It is staffed by warders and a governor, and there are prisoners in 1870 period uniform.

The atmosphere in the jail is surreal: a fifteen-man jury, solicitors, witnesses and the accused sandwiched between two burly policemen – but they are all dummies.

Visitors can try out a hard labour machine and make traditional herring nets as prisoners did a century and more ago. The Crime and Punishment exhibition has gory details of medieval punishments, hangings, brandings, tongue borings and burnings. Definitely not for the squeamish!

Facilities include a shop and limited access for wheelchairs.

Property	**JARLSHOF**
Location	Sumburgh Head, Shetland
Status	SDD
Open	0930–1900, Sun 1400–1900, closed winter
Admission	Nominal charge, reduced rate for children & senior citizens
Phone	0950 60112

Jarlshof is one of the most amazing archaeological sites in Europe with a complex of ancient settlements within three acres. The villages were occupied from the Bronze Age until Viking times. Such a walk through prehistory and history is not possible anywhere else in Britain.

Fragments of a house dated between 1500 and 2000 BC can be seen. There is a Bronze Age village of oval stone huts, and an Iron Age broch and wheelhouses. There is a Norse settlement, a number of farms from the ninth to the 13th centuries, and on the crest of a mound there is a house which was built around 1600.

It was not until the 19th century that Jarlshof aroused interest again when Sir Walter Scott used the ruins for his description of the house of Mr Mertoun in *The Pirate*.

There are no facilities for disabled people.

Property	**OFFICIAL LOCH NESS MONSTER EXHIBITION CENTRE**
Location	Drumnadrochit, Inverness, Highland
Status	Private
Open	Easter–31 May, 0930–1730; 1 Jun–30 Jun, 0900–2000; 1 July–10 Sep, 0900–2130; 11 Sep–31 Oct, 0930–2000
Admission	Nominal charge, reduced rate for children & senior citizens
Phone	045 62 218/573/202

The prows of Norse longships bore the sea dragon as a figurehead, and Viking legends tell of strange creatures in northern waters. St Columba is said to have been the first person to spot 'Nessie' and there have been several alleged sightings since 1933.

The Loch Ness Phenomena Investigation Bureau was set up in 1962 to organise further research and collate evidence, and lasted for ten years. Then the Academy of Applied Science took over. This was followed in turn by the Loch Ness Project and Operation Deepscan. But there is no conclusive proof of the existence of a monster . . . yet.

The exhibition centre has a large multi-media presentation, and the equipment that has been used to try to trace the beast is on display. There are shops, craft demonstrations, a restaurant and hotel with access and facilities for disabled people.

Property	**SCOTCH WHISKY HERITAGE CENTRE**
Location	Next to Edinburgh Castle
Status	Private
Open	1000–1700, extended during summer
Admission	Nominal charge, reduced rate for children & senior citizens
Phone	031 220 0441

The winner of a British Tourist Authority Come to Britain award, this visitor centre stands at the top of the historic Royal Mile. It brings to life the story of smugglers and Scotch whisky in an interesting fashion. There are guided tours and an audio-visual show. Visitors seated on converted whisky barrels are transported through the centuries and told about 'the water of life'. There are tell-tale sounds and aromas, and visitors can listen to Robert Burns lament the closure of his favourite distillery. There is a commentary in English, Dutch, French, German, Italian, Japanese and Spanish.

There is a blender's laboratory and a bonded warehouse with the distillery cat. A gift shop sells over 60 brands of whisky.

Wheelchair access, a lift and a toilet for disabled people are available.

Property	**SKARA BRAE**
Location	19 m NW of Kirkwall, Orkney
Status	SDD
Open	Summer: 0930–1900, Sun, 1400–1600 Winter: 0930–1600, Sun 1400–1900
Admission	Nominal charge, reduced rate for children & senior citizens
Phone	0856 84815

Skara Brae, the best preserved group of Stone Age
houses in Western Europe, lay buried in drift sand for
4500 years until it was revealed by a storm in 1850.

This neolithic village was inhabited before the
Pyramids were built, and some of its structures remain
impressively intact. Nowhere else in Northern Europe
is there Stone Age furniture in such a good state of
preservation. The sand, and the midden which
surrounded the village, helped preserve it for posterity.

Skara Brae was probably occupied from 3000 BC
until 2700 BC, and stone beds, fireplaces, dressers and
cupboards have survived. The villagers were part of a
close-knit community of farmers and herds who
cremated their deceased relatives in tombs. The
remains give a fascinating insight into how people lived
in prehistoric times.

Facilities include a visitor centre. Guide dogs are
allowed, but there is no access for wheelchairs.

USEFUL ADDRESSES

Countryside Commission for Scotland, Battleby, Redgorton, Perth, PH1 3EW (0738 27921)

Historic Buildings and Monuments (SDD), 20, Brandon Street, Edinburgh, EH3 5RA (031 556 8400)

National Museums of Scotland, York Buildings, Queen Street, Edinburgh, EH2 1JD (031 225 7534)

National Trust for Scotland, 5, Charlotte Square, Edinburgh, EH2 4DU (031 226 5922)

Nature Conservancy Council, 12, Hope Terrace, Edinburgh, EH9 2AS (031 447 4784)

Ramblers' Association, Kelinbank, Freuchie, Fife, KY7 7EP (0337 58065)

Scotland's Gardens Scheme, 31 Castle Terrace, Edinburgh, EH1 2EL (031 229 1870)

Scottish Arts Council, 12, Manor Place, Edinburgh, EH3 7DD (031 226 6051)

Scottish Museums Council, 20–22, Torphichen Street, Edinburgh, EH3 8JB (031 229 7465)

Scottish Rights of Way Society Ltd, 1, Lutton Place, Edinburgh, EH8 9PD (031 447 9242)

Scottish Tourist Board, 23, Ravelston Terrace, Edinburgh, EH4 3EU (031 332 2433)

Scottish Wildlife Trust, 25, Johnston Terrace, Edinburgh, EH1 2NH (031 226 4602)

Scottish Youth Hostels' Association, 7, Glebe Crescent, Stirling, FK8 2JA (07865 1181)

INDEX